PUBLISHED BY AMERICAN HERITAGE PUBLISHING CO., INC.

BOOK TRADE AND INSTITUTIONAL DISTRIBUTION BY
HARPER & ROW

FIRST EDITION

© 1970 by American Heritage Publishing Co., Inc.,
551 Fifth Avenue, New York, New York 10017.
All rights reserved under Berne and Pan-American
Copyright Conventions. Library of Congress Catalog
Card Number: 73–105906.
Standard Book Number: (trade edition) 8281–5029–X;
(library edition) 8281–8027–X.
Trademark AMERICAN HERITAGE JUNIOR LIBRARY
registered United States Patent Office.

FRANKLIN DELANO ROOSEVELT

BY THE EDITORS OF AMERICAN HERITAGE *The Magazine of History*

AUTHOR WILSON SULLIVAN

CONSULTANT FRANK FREIDEL
Professor of History, Harvard University

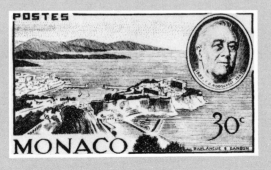

Monaco, El Salvador, and of course the United States were among the many countries that issued postage stamps commemorating Franklin Delano Roosevelt, a dedicated philatelist from his youth.

FOREWORD

1535436

At the age of thirty-nine Franklin Delano Roosevelt was a politician with a promising future, but he hardly appeared destined for greatness. He had passed blandly through an exclusive boarding school, Harvard College, and Columbia Law School without either distinction or disgrace. He had survived the attentions of a doting mother to become a good husband to the distant cousin he had married and a kind father to the five children she had borne him. He was a good sportsman with a special fondness for the sea, a sometime lawyer, a former Assistant Secretary of the Navy, and the recent loser of the Vice-Presidency to his Republican opponent. "Pleasant," Henry Cabot Lodge called him, "a well-meaning, nice young fellow, but light."

Then, in the summer of 1921, Roosevelt was struck down by polio. It was the great turning point in his life, for as his paralyzed legs withered, his character grew stronger, refined by pain and by the unaccustomed physical dependence on others. The old frivolity gave way to concern; the old arrogance, to understanding. And with a new sense of commitment, he stubbornly refused to relinquish politics for the idle, comfortable life of a rich invalid.

From the time he was elected Governor of New York in 1928 to his death during his fourth term as President of the United States, Franklin Roosevelt fought as hard from his chair as any boxer in the ring to make his political philosophy a reality. "Government," he once said, "has a final responsibility for the well-being of its citizenship." Action, not talk; experiment, not theory were the guiding principles behind F.D.R.'s legislative New Deal, which was unprecedented in its originality.

Hardly had America survived the great Depression of the thirties when it was plunged into global war. Roosevelt's and the nation's enemy was no longer poverty but tyranny, and once again his sure hand led Americans to victory.

The private citizen and the public servant, the scion of Hyde Park and the diplomat of Casablanca, Teheran, and Yalta all are represented in this revealing biography, which traces the development of a remarkable American aristocrat who lent his name to an era.

THE EDITORS

RIGHT: *This 1932 campaign license plate was also a guide to pronouncing the candidate's name.*
STANLEY KING COLLECTION

COVER: *The President happily gives reporters a tour of his estate at Hyde Park in 1937.*
FRANKLIN DELANO ROOSEVELT LIBRARY, HYDE PARK

FRONT ENDSHEET: *Pittsburghers for F.D.R. in 1932 wanted an end to Prohibition and Hoover.*
UPI

TITLE PAGE: *Hoover and Roosevelt prepare to ride together to F.D.R.'s first inauguration.*
WIDE WORLD PHOTOS, NEW YORK

BACK ENDSHEET: *A hatless Roosevelt ignored the rain while delivering his second inaugural.*
UPI

BACK COVER: *F.D.R. always wore this hat campaigning for he felt that it brought him luck.*
FRANKLIN DELANO ROOSEVELT LIBRARY

CONTENTS

1

"A BEAUTIFUL FRAME"

President Grover Cleveland looked down solemnly at his five-year-old White House visitor. "My little man," he declared, "I am making a strange wish for you. I hope that you may never be President of the United States!"

For many years Franklin Delano Roosevelt gave very little indication that he would deny Cleveland his wish. He had been born, on January 30, 1882, in Hyde Park, New York, to every privilege of wealth. As a youth he lived in a mansion in which it was considered bad taste even to discuss money. His boyhood was like a page from a picture book, free of shadows. "He was brought up," an aunt recalled, "in a beautiful frame," in gilded isolation from the harsh realities of life. At his mother's insistence, his mind had been kept "on nice

Franklin Delano Roosevelt at the age of sixteen months perches rather tentatively on the shoulder of his proud father, James.

things, at a high level," on dancing school, on frequent trips to Europe, on lessons given by private tutors, on swimming and yachting off Campobello in Canada, where his mother had purchased a summer estate, because, she explained, "it will be good for Franklin."

Franklin's mother, Sara Delano Roosevelt, whose Flemish ancestors settled in America in 1621, left few areas of her only child's life unsupervised: she even advised him on how to make his signature more distinguished. Sara saved everything Franklin ever touched, and when he came down with scarlet fever, she rushed back from a European holiday and defied the doctor's quarantine by climbing a ladder to her son's window, where she engaged him in comforting conversation. She might bring him to task for ordering his playmates about, but she no doubt took pride in his confident reply: "Mummie, if I didn't give the orders, nothing would happen." And she knew how to handle him. Once,

The Roosevelts' house at Hyde Park was set in the midst of an orderly estate overlooking the Hudson. It is now a National Historic Site administered by the Department of the Interior.

when Franklin expressed the desire to come and go as he pleased, Sara announced that on the following day he could do precisely that. The next evening, repentant and tired after a day of hungry liberty, the boy slipped more than willingly back into his mother's routine.

Despite her doting, however, Sara Roosevelt expected surprisingly little of her son. That he should become President or go into "public life of any sort," she later insisted, was "the last thing I should ever have imagined for him." She hoped only that he would "grow to be like his father, straight and honorable, just and kind, an upstanding American."

James Roosevelt's influence on his son was less decisive. "Poughkeepsie Jimmy," who enjoyed the luxury of his own railway car, had his hands full managing extensive interests in shipping, coal, and farming. He was twice as old as his wife, and in his mutton-chop whiskers and tweeds, was the very model of the Dutch country squire. He taught his son riding and other gentlemanly arts. He bought him his first gun at eleven, with which Franklin shot one each of the scores of local Dutchess County birds to

start a collection that became out-
standing. James taught him how to
sail and instilled in his son a lifelong
love of the sea.

James also had—and imparted to
Franklin—a keen sense of the Roosevelts' social position. Rejecting the
hospitality of their newly rich neighbors the Vanderbilts, James explained
to his wife: "But don't you see, Sallie,
that if we accept their invitation, then
we shall have to invite them to our
house." James also was active in politics, and his standing in the Democratic Party prompted President Grover Cleveland to offer him a diplomatic

TEXT CONTINUED ON PAGE 16

*Franklin's mother, Sara, had been married
a year when this picture was taken in 1881.*

AN ENVIABLE CHILDHOOD

James Roosevelt taught young Franklin everything that a gentleman had to know, while his mother recorded her only son's progress in her daily diary. It was an enviable childhood, replete with governesses, tutors, sports, horses and pet dogs, trips to Europe and to Campobello. At Hyde Park, the family's comfortable estate on the Hudson, the gates were closed to the problems that Franklin would face later as the thirty-second President of the United States.

At the age of three, above, Franklin promenaded with a dog on the family burro. At nine, below, the young sailor began to cultivate his enduring love for the sea.

At sixteen, above, the boy took his own picture by using an early self-timing device. Below, the landlocked sailor looks as though he would much rather be afloat.

The eleven-year-old F.D.R. had his own riding rig and the assured air of a most capable equestrian.

28-39 Franklin's first report.

GROTON SCHOOL,
GROTON, MASS.

Report of F. Roosevelt III
for the month ending Oct. 17 - 1896
Rank in Class of 19 Boys — 4

		MONTHLY AVERAGE	EXAMINATION MARKS
Latin,		7.2.0	
	Composition,		
Greek,		6.2.2	
	Composition,		
Mathematics,	Trigonometry,		
	Geometry,		
	Algebra,	9.7+	
	Arithmetic,		
English,	Literature,		
	Composition,		
	Grammar,		
	Reading,		
French,			
German,			
History,		7.73	
Science,		9.00	
Physics,			
Sacred Studies,			
Punctuality,		10.00	
Neatness,		9.66	
Decorum,			
AVERAGE MARK FOR THE MONTH,		7.14	
AVERAGE MARK FOR THE TERM,			

REMARKS. Very good. He strikes me as an intelligent & faithful scholar & a good boy.
E. Peabody

From the Groton years Sara saved Franklin's first report, in which the headmaster calls him "an intelligent and faithful scholar and a good boy," and the letter justifying his failure of a Greek examination.

Sunday
Oct. 3rd 1897

My dear Papa and Mama,
I forgot to mention in my last letter, that I, together with many others had had the great pleasure of failing the most outrageous Greek exam, which has ever been known in the history of education. Not only was the paper unfair but the marking was atrocious, and altho' I got about 30 the old idiot Abbott refused to ... as by several fellows and he is generally liked ... With a great deal of love to both of you & hugs & kisses F. D. Roosevelt

---

TEXT CONTINUED FROM PAGE 13

post abroad. It was during his father's visit to the White House to decline this post that Franklin met the President and heard his ironic wish.

Franklin went to Groton, the distinguished boarding school, when he was fourteen, having been enrolled there at the age of two by his mother. Under the tutelage of the Rev. Endicott Peabody, young F.D.R. learned Groton's primary lesson: that it was the responsibility of the wealthy and privileged classes to aid—and lead—the less fortunate. Roosevelt doesn't seem to have suffered unduly under Groton's Spartan regimen for the de-

velopment of gentlemanly Christian character: cold showers before breakfast, compulsory chapel, strict punctuality, and stiff collars and patent leather shoes at dinner. He played Uncle Bopaddy in the school's production of W. S. Gilbert's *The Wedding March*, sang in the choir, and like his distant cousin Teddy, took boxing lessons. He was not heavy enough to play on the baseball team, but he did become team manager.

Although F.D.R. won a prize in Latin, he did not overtax his brain, reporting to "Papa and Mama" on one occasion his "great pleasure of

16

failing the most outrageous Greek exam which has ever been known in the history of education." His teacher, he declared, was an "old idiot," and he announced his intention to "assasinate" (sic) him if he failed to pass him again, "as I know the whole book by heart." Even though he was the only Democrat in a school of 150 boys, Roosevelt did not stand out from the crowd. He struck one classmate as "nice but colorless." The Rev.

Peabody remembered his pupil as "a quiet, satisfactory boy of more than ordinary intelligence, . . . but not brilliant."

After Groton, Roosevelt intended to enroll in the Naval Academy at Annapolis, but he was overruled by his father, who suggested that the study of law would be more suitable and take him less far from home. F.D.R. therefore entered Harvard in 1900, the year in which his father died.

In Franklin's senior year the Groton class play was The Wedding March. *In his father's top hat and tails the young Roosevelt (right) plays Uncle Bopaddy, a role he was delighted to take.*

But even there the future leader of the Western alliance, as one colleague observed, showed "almost no awareness whatever of realities beyond the undergraduate horizon." Roosevelt was crushed when Harvard's snootiest club, the Porcellian, refused him admission and equally hurt when he found that he was too light for the football team. Occupying a suite in one of Harvard's most fashionable houses—chosen and decorated by his mother, who had moved to Boston to be near her son after James Roosevelt died—Roosevelt was content with a casual "C" average. In later life, however, he liked to dangle an honorary Phi Beta Kappa key from his vest-pocket chain.

Six-foot-one and lithe at 146 pounds, with a proud, handsome, almost classic face, a pointed chin, and thin, prim lips, Roosevelt cut an elegant figure striding through Harvard Yard, driving through Cambridge in his runabout, or throwing after-the-atre parties for selected friends in Harvard's prep school clique. He was, as one biographer writes, "a happy, average, well-bred young man," of immense charm, but little idealism and social awareness. Even as editor of *The Crimson*, the college's distinguished undergraduate newspaper, Roosevelt's concerns remained petty:

For twenty-year-old Franklin after his sophomore year at Harvard, a happy summer was a shady garden and a pretty girl to tease.

the need for better walks on college grounds and "constant support" for the football team "from every member of the University."

Showing little of the liberal thinking of his later years, he joined the Republican Club and marched in a torchlight parade for William McKinley and cousin Teddy. F.D.R. helped organize a student committee to raise funds for the Boers, and in an essay, urged Southern colleges to follow Harvard's example of admitting Negroes. But in general he toed the conservative line of his peers. After Teddy became President, Franklin deplored his firm settlement of a perilous coal strike as an unwarranted subordination of the Congress to the Executive. As a sophomore, he attacked those of his ancestors who had done nothing while the community suffered, but he gave little indication that he planned to lift his own hand in its behalf.

When he was still only a junior at Harvard, Roosevelt shocked his mother by announcing his desire to marry Eleanor Roosevelt, a distant cousin whom he had known since childhood and met again at a recent family dance. Despite her son's assurance that Eleanor had "a very good mind," Sara set out to thwart the marriage. She bundled Franklin off on a West Indies cruise, and even his shipboard flirtation with a fetching Frenchwoman struck Sara as preferable to the impending marriage. Wasn't Eleanor known even in the

Eleanor held Franklin's hat and pretended to read the paper while he snapped this picture during a gondola ride they took in Venice while honeymooning in the summer of 1905.

family as socially awkward, even something of an ugly duckling? Eleanor's own mother had nicknamed her Granny.

Sara's opposition lost out to love. When Franklin, then a student at Columbia University Law School, reminded his fiancée that professionally he had "only a few bright prospects now," Eleanor had replied serenely: "I'm sure you will really amount to something someday." F.D.R. assured Sara in a letter that "nothing can ever change what we have always been & always will be to each other," but he and Eleanor were married in New York on March 17, 1905. President Teddy, who was in town to review the Saint Patrick's Day parade, "greatly rejoiced" about the marriage and gave the bride away. After a brief first honeymoon in Hyde Park the couple returned to New York, where Franklin finished out his first year at the Columbia Law School. In the summer of 1905 the newlyweds went on a grand tour of Europe.

The honeymoon ended in more ways than one when Franklin and his bride returned home to discover that Sara intended to rule their household as though it were her own, with no opposition from Franklin. Sara ordered two adjoining houses built on East 65th Street in New York and overruled Eleanor at every turn. She hired and supervised her son and daughter-in-law's servants, ordered their furniture, and exercised to the fullest the financial control over Franklin that

Soon after the Roosevelts' marriage, Franklin and friends were snapped wading at Campobello.

James had requested in his will. Sara even chose the clothes and toys for her grandchildren: Anna, or "Sis," who would accompany her father on his fateful trip to Yalta; Jimmy, destined to be Roosevelt's chief White House aide and a progressive Congressman; rebellious Elliott, who would reject Harvard and later engage in ranching and mining in the West; Franklin, Jr., a lawyer and liberal Congressman; and John, who first would shock Sara by working in a Boston department store and then would split the Hyde Park Roosevelts by becoming a Wall Street Republican.

Eleanor faltered under Sara's domination. "I do not like living in a house that is in no way mine," she said tearfully to F.D.R., "one which I have done nothing about and does not represent the way I want to live." Roosevelt, failing utterly to understand, replied: "You are quite mad."

21

Assistant Secretary of the Navy Roosevelt stands at far right during Flag Day ceremonies in Washington in 1913. At left are William J. Bryan, Josephus Daniels, and Woodrow Wilson.

Admitted to the bar after leaving Columbia in 1907, Roosevelt joined the firm of Carter, Ledyard, and Milburn. Shortly thereafter, financed by his mother, he opened and soon closed his own office. He was bored by the law, but he became fascinated by politics. In 1910, at only twenty-eight,

Roosevelt was approached by Dutchess County Democratic leaders to run for the state legislature. When he explained that he would have to check with Sara, a party chieftain replied: "Frank, there are men back in Poughkeepsie waiting for your answer. They won't like to hear you had to ask your

22

mother." Nevertheless, Sara was consulted and so, too, indirectly, was Franklin's cousin Teddy.

In Republican Dutchess County the word "Democrat" had the scent of original sin. Yet F.D.R., the Democratic candidate, barnstormed through the district in a dashing, red, two-cylinder Maxwell decked out with flags and banners. He promised a reformed Democratic Party, free of the corruption of Tammany Hall, and he committed himself to fight for a standardized apple barrel, which perhaps meant more to his rural audiences. Jimmy Roosevelt's son looked awfully out of place in his rounded stiff collar, high-buttoned shoes, British suits, and pince-nez spectacles. But tired of Republican rule in Albany and impressed by Roosevelt's famous name, Dutchess County elected its second Democratic state senator in over fifty years.

Roosevelt had barely warmed his Senate seat in Albany when he was embroiled in a battle with party regulars. By leading a band of insurgents against the selection of a Tammany hack for the United States Senate, F.D.R. became known as a reformer but won few friends among party officials. "So we've got another Roosevelt!" snorted party boss "Big Tim" Sullivan, who recalled cousin Teddy's days in Albany with distaste. "Wouldn't it be better to drown him before he grows up?" Nor were political drones like Sullivan alone in their aversion to this upstart from the apple country. A

social worker named Frances Perkins, whom F.D.R., as President, would appoint as the nation's first woman Secretary of Labor, condemned young Franklin's arrogance, self-righteousness, and his "deafness to the hopes, fears, and aspirations which are the common lot." She particularly disliked his failure to support actively a bill limiting New York's work week for women to fifty-four hours. "No one who saw him in those years," she concluded, "would have been likely to think of him as a potential President of the U.S.A."

Even Louis McHenry Howe, a reporter whose devotion to Roosevelt, the President, was legendary, found him at first "a spoiled, silk-pants sort of a guy." F.D.R. would confess later that he "was an awfully mean cuss when I first went into politics." But in Albany he was oblivious to criticism; he was having, after all, more "fun," as he put it, than ever before in his life. "With his handsome face and his form of supple strength," *The New York Times* reported, "he could make a fortune on the stage and set the matinee girl's heart throbbing with subtle and happy emotion." In 1912, with Howe organizing a skillful campaign, F.D.R. was re-elected by a greatly increased majority.

Even then Roosevelt was attracting the notice of noted politicians. In 1911 he had struck Woodrow Wilson, then Governor of New Jersey, as "the handsomest young giant I have ever seen," and at the Democratic Na-

tional Convention of 1912 Franklin helped swing the vital New York delegation to Wilson on the 46th ballot. His grasp of political realities greatly impressed Josephus Daniels, soon to be named Wilson's Secretary of the Navy. "It was a case of love at first sight," Daniels later recalled. He found young Roosevelt "a clean-living athlete, an ambitious, upstanding, and highminded young man."

At fifteen, Roosevelt—the skipper of his own twenty-one-foot knockabout—already had read Mahan's *The Influence of Sea Power Upon History* and was in his own words "crazy" about the sea. Thus a dream came true, when, on March 17, 1913—his eighth wedding anniversary—he was sworn in as Wilson's Assistant Secretary of the Navy. At thirty-one he was the youngest man ever to hold the post, and he heard promptly from his proud cousin Teddy: "It is interesting to see," wrote the former President, "that you are in another place which I myself once held."

Even in high national office, F.D.R. lost none of his old gaiety. In an official memorandum to Secretary Daniels he solemnly announced: " I beg to report . . . that I have just signed a requisition (with 4 copies attached) calling for purchase of 8 Carpet Tacks." And his boss replied on cue: "Why this wanton extravagance? I am sure that two would suffice."

During a tour of American naval bases in Europe in 1918, Franklin Roosevelt proved to be an active Assistant Secretary. Here he walks the plank to shore from his seaplane.

But relations between Daniels and F.D.R. were somewhat strained from the outset. Neither the Secretary nor the Navy Department, Roosevelt was convinced, was really aware of the peril posed by the Kaiser's Germany, or indeed, of the revolutionary nature of modern warfare. When war broke out in Europe in 1914, Roosevelt wrote to Eleanor that everyone was "apparently utterly oblivious to the fact that the most terrible drama in history was about to be enacted." He ridiculed the pacifist Daniels as "the funniest looking hillbilly I have ever seen." He mocked the Secretary's sadness when events, as F.D.R. said, shattered Daniels' "faith in human nature and civilization and similar idealistic nonsense. . . ." To Eleanor he boasted: "I am *running* the real work, although Josephus is here. He is bewildered by it all but very sweet and sad."

For all his bravado, Roosevelt was an energetic Assistant Secretary and his policies helped build up the American fleet for World War I. He was instrumental in laying the famous North Sea Mine Barrage, a 240-mile curtain of mines stretching from Scotland to Norway, designed to check German U-boat assaults on Allied shipping. He favored a similar network of mines to protect the English Channel. An irrepressible activist and believer in preparedness, he worked hard for reform in American Navy yards, personally toured the war zone and U.S. bases overseas, and attended the Versailles Peace Conference as an observer for the Navy Department. Before the war's end he had met Britain's Minister of Munitions, Winston Churchill, for the first but by no means the last time.

Always impulsive, Roosevelt had little regard for formalities. He undertook multimillion-dollar projects without Congressional approval, saw nothing inappropriate in personally landing with the Marines to quell a revolution in Haiti, even borrowed a Navy destroyer to speed him to his summer retreat at Campobello. He begged Wilson for an assignment to active duty at sea and was deterred only by the President's insistence that he was of more value to the Allied cause in Washington.

As an administrator, however, Roosevelt demonstrated talent and style. He became more adroit in the tactics of persuasion, and if his farewell letter to Secretary Daniels can be accepted at face value, he grew less impetuous: "You have taught me so wisely and kept my feet on the ground when I was about to skyrocket. . . ." F.D.R. resigned his post on August 6, 1920.

During his tenure in the Navy Department, Roosevelt had run unsuccessfully in the 1914 New York Democratic primary for nomination to the United States Senate. His defeat was due largely to the efforts of an unforgiving Tammany Hall. In 1920 he faced his second and last defeat at the polls. During the Democratic Con-

UNDER WHICH FLAG?

Whether or not the United States should join the League of Nations became a 1920 campaign issue. Democratic candidate James M. Cox (left, above) was for it, while Republican Warren G. Harding opposed it and won. Below, Cox and Roosevelt campaign in Dayton, Ohio.

vention of that year he delighted his children by grabbing the New York standard from Tammany henchmen who refused to demonstrate for the ailing President Wilson when his portrait was unveiled. Defiantly he raised the flag in a gesture of loyalty to the Chief Executive who had been broken by his losing fight for the League of Nations. Roosevelt also seconded the nomination of his controversial friend Al Smith for the Presidency, but the convention chose the more moderate Governor James M. Cox of Ohio.

To the surprise of many delegates, Cox said he wanted Franklin D. Roosevelt as his running mate. Cox later confessed that "so far as I knew, I had never seen him; but I explained . . . that he met the geographical requirement, that he was recognized as an independent and that Roosevelt was a well-known name." After a speech by Al Smith praising Roosevelt's wartime service in the Navy Department, F.D.R. was nominated for the Vice-Presidency by acclamation, an honor that appears to have taken the thirty-eight-year-old politician by surprise.

To party strategists Cox and Roosevelt made an ideal team. On the prohibition issue, Cox was wet, Roosevelt dry. On the divisive issue of the League of Nations, which the Democratic Party platform favored as "the surest, if not the only, practicable means of maintaining the permanent peace . . . ," Cox had been lukewarm, Roosevelt enthusiastic. But the men got on well during the campaign, a

major exception being Cox's refusal to grant Roosevelt's request that he be permitted to sit in on Cabinet meetings if elected. Cox felt that such a practice might make the Senate suspect that its presiding officer was "a White House snoop."

The campaign trail was heady stuff for the young Roosevelt. This was the first election in which women were permitted to vote, and with Eleanor at his side—as a symbol of women's newly won freedom—the Hyde Park matinee idol was mobbed by the fair sex. Flashing his famous grin, he shouted to the crowds he adored: "Come and see me some time!"

It was a grueling schedule, some 800 speeches in 42 states, supporting Wilson's League of Nations in hamlets that probably had never heard of it. F.D.R. also emphasized the theme of his eloquent acceptance speech: that there must be an end to "mere coma" in national life and that a revitalized federal government must be at least as effective as a business concern in meeting people's needs. "Some people," he had declared in accepting the nomination, "have been saying of late: 'We are tired of progress, we want to go back to where we were before; . . . to restore 'normal' conditions.' They are wrong. This is not the wish of America. We can never go back. The good old days are gone past forever."

The campaign offered F.D.R. a chance to see America in a unique way. Spending 89 out of 92 days aboard a train, he "got to know the country as only a candidate for national office or a traveling salesman can get to know it." And he promised, if elected, to "put the job of Vice-President on the map for the first time in history." He never got the chance. Appealing for a return to "normalcy" in an America weary of war and international involvement, Warren G. Harding and Calvin Coolidge triumphed with a staggering plurality of more than seven million votes.

On the surface, at least, Roosevelt accepted his defeat with philosophic good cheer. "Thank God," he told campaign aide Stephen T. Early of the Associated Press, "we are both comparatively youthful." But F.D.R. had braced himself. His son Jimmy reports that Roosevelt "knew before the campaign ended that the cause was hopeless." His mother wrote in her diary: "Rainy day. . . . Franklin rather relieved not to be elected. . . ." But to anyone who had watched Roosevelt on the campaign trail it was clear that Sara was speaking for herself. Even in defeat F.D.R. had become a national figure. He was more poised in meeting simple people, more confident of his grasp of the issues, more skilled and effective as a public speaker. He had lost the battle, not the war.

In July, 1920, Democratic vice-presidential candidate Roosevelt strolled through Washington waving, smiling, and looking as though he would win the election he lost.

HARRIS & EWING: GILLOON PHOTO AGENCY, NEW YORK

2

"NO SOB STUFF"

Once more a private citizen, at thirty-eight, Roosevelt insisted that he was "delighted to get back to real work again." He had formed a law partnership with Grenville T. Emmet and Langdon P. Martin and also had been made vice-president in charge of the New York office of the Fidelity and Deposit Company of Maryland, then the third largest bonding firm in the nation. His total income, including his inheritance, was about $50,000.

Roosevelt was bored by both jobs, however, and throughout the booming 1920's he satisfied his need for excitement by speculating in the stock of a wild variety of half-baked businesses. Despite the protests of his mother and wife, he plunged into a wildcat oil venture in Wyoming. When his drills struck not oil but gas, he suffered heavy losses. He foundered again by backing the dirigible rather than the airplane as the air transport of the future. Later, he invested in a clerkless store that sold small things, such as candy and razor blades, from automatic machines. This ill-fated adventure would come back to haunt him in the Depression years when he was campaigning for more jobs for the poor.

During their courtship Eleanor had introduced her fiancé to the squalor of slum tenements and the hardships of the poor. Now, true to the code that he had learned at Groton, Roosevelt took a paternal interest in public causes. He served as chairman of the Greater New York Committee of the Boy Scouts of America, and he raised funds for the Seaman's Church Institute for needy sailors and for the Lighthouse for the Blind. He helped to create the Woodrow Wilson Foundation to subsidize students of international affairs.

Roosevelt and his family sat for this portrait in 1919. The children, left to right, are: Anna, thirteen; Franklin, Jr., five, on his father's knee; James, twelve; John, three, on his mother's knee; Elliot, six.

TEXT CONTINUED ON PAGE 34

A RUGGED ISLAND

As a child and as a father, Roosevelt summered on the Canadian island of Campobello off Eastport, Maine. Sailing the treacherous Bay of Fundy was the principal sport, but also there were croquet, golf, and occasionally dangerous games of follow-the-leader over the sea-washed rocks. Franklin adored every moment of it, although Eleanor noted: "Quite a number of persons really did not enjoy Father's games at all." It was at Campobello, in August, 1921, that polio struck F.D.R.

Boating in all forms was a Roosevelt passion at Campobello. A year before he was stricken with polio, F.D.R. posed with his sons James (left) and Elliot on the Vireo, *the smaller of the family's two sailboats. Below, a younger Franklin paddles his canoe on the Bay of Fundy.*

From Campobello the view of the Bay of Fundy is so broad that Franklin's cousin Laura Delano was obliged to join three photographs in order to make the composite panorama above. Abundant picnics by the shore, like the one below that Eleanor (standing, right) organized, were among the many things that the Roosevelts did as a family during their summers on the island.

All the while, Roosevelt never neglected politics. He saw the weakness of local Democratic organizations and the political "me-tooism" that had helped defeat him and Cox in 1920. Determined to forge a strong state and national party, Roosevelt corresponded constantly with Democratic leaders, seeking a platform that would unite all Democrats. His own star had risen, even in defeat, and despite his conviction that the Senate was the cemetery of politicians, he refused to discount rumors that he might seek a Senate seat in 1922.

Weekends at Hyde Park were enlivened by picnics, model boat racing, and the general good cheer of the tightly knit Roosevelt clan. Like his father before him, Franklin relished the life of the country squire: hunting, golfing, elegant parties, and high teas. He reveled above all in the challenge of sailing off his beloved Campobello, defying the treacherous waters of the Bay of Fundy with that proud toss of the head for which millions would remember him. To his son Jimmy, "Pa-*pa*" was simply "the handsomest, strongest, most glamorous, vigorous, physical father in the world."

A perennial adolescent, F.D.R. loved a good joke, the more daring and zany the better. At the height of Prohibition he "caught" a New York City police commissioner red-handed taking a nip. F.D.R., the commissioner, and a group of friends were passing around the forbidden alcohol, which someone thoughtfully had concealed in a hollow cane. As the police official lifted the cane to his lips, Roosevelt appointed himself "prosecuting attorney." Sampling the liquor himself, F.D.R. announced with mock solemnity: "May it please the court, I find that the liquid in this container is nothing more than vanilla extract, and I move that the case be dismissed."

At the end of July, 1921, Roosevelt sailed to Campobello for a much needed rest. He could not know that it was to be his last trip to the island for twelve years; that his "vacation" would change world history.

Fishing for cod off the island on August 9, Roosevelt fell overboard into the frigid waters of the Bay of Fundy. "I'd never felt anything so cold as that water!" Roosevelt recalled. "I hardly went under, hardly wet my head, because I still had hold of the side of the tender, but the water was so cold it seemed paralyzing."

The next day F.D.R., James, Anna, and Elliott, again sailing, spotted a forest fire on a nearby island. They landed, put out the fire with evergreen branches, and then dogtrotted to a lake one and a half miles away. The swim failed to cool F.D.R., and he plunged again into the icy bay. Back home, still in his wet bathing suit, Roosevelt read his mail and his newspapers. Suddenly he was seized by a profound chill and a stab of pain. He went to bed early, announcing that he had suffered a spell of lumbago.

"The next morning," Roosevelt remembered, "when I swung out of bed my left leg lagged but I managed to move about and to shave. I tried to persuade myself that the trouble with my leg was muscular, that it would disappear as I used it. But presently it refused to work, and then the other."

Then an incredible tragedy of errors began. Despite Roosevelt's acute pain and paralysis, a doctor summoned from nearby Lubec, Maine, said that his patient had no more than an old-fashioned cold. Within two days the paralysis had spread to Roosevelt's chest and fingers, and three days later, a specialist was called in. He announced that a blood clot from "a sudden congestion had settled in the lower spinal cord, removing the power to move." He prescribed and Eleanor and the faithful Howe administered sustained deep massage, further damaging the future President's leg muscles.

The truth was not known until August 25. Franklin Delano Roosevelt, at the age of thirty-nine, had acute anterior poliomyelitis—infantile paralysis.

For days he was feverish, suffering indescribable pain, his nerves so raw that hoops had to be placed between his body and his bedclothes. For several days Roosevelt's arms and chest, even his eyes, seemed in danger.

No one, least of all Roosevelt and the doctors who first treated him, had realized that he would never walk, stand, or sit down unaided again. Until his death, he could never be left alone, except in sleep—and then only

with an attendant nearby. His confident stride would give way to steel braces, a wheelchair, crutches, and cane. He would be lifted and carried about, his legs now lifeless and as thin as a child's.

F.D.R. was haunted by inner fears, but he gave no outward hint that he suspected the truth, and he flashed his famous grin to comfort his family and friends. "He has such courage, such ambition," a doctor said, "and yet at the same time such an extraordinarily sensitive emotional mechanism that it will take all the skill which we can muster to lead him successfully to a recognition of what he really faces without crushing him."

Everyone had underestimated Roosevelt's hard Dutch courage. "No sob stuff," he would tell inquiring reporters in later years. And now, in what John Gunther has called a "conquest of flesh by will and spirit," Roosevelt began his long journey back, a treasured poem giving him strength:

> In the full clutch of circumstance,
> I have not winced, nor cried out loud,
> And under the bludgeonings of chance
> My head is bloody but unbowed.
>
> It matters not how strait the gate,
> How charged with punishment the
>   scroll,
> I am the master of my fate,
> I am the captain of my soul.

He was helped, too, by a quiet religious faith. He was never to be a first-pew Episcopal churchman. But there can be no doubt that an inner spiritual confidence, nurtured at Groton under the Rev. Endicott Peabody, sustained him in those first bitter moments when he was forced to admit the seriousness of his condition.

By late October, 1921, Roosevelt had returned to his New York City home, determined to walk again. In the months that followed, he crawled from room to room on his hands and knees, panting and sweating but never asking for help. Hand-over-hand up the banister he dragged himself up to his room, his dead legs trailing. He stood courageously erect, his legs locked in steel braces that were strapped around his waist, jointed and clamped at the knees, and fastened into the heels of his shoes. At Hyde Park he tried daily to make the long walk to the gate, often failing, but never ceasing to try. In every possible way he tried to shield his children from the grim truth about the father whom they had idolized for physical strength and prowess. At great risk, he wrestled with them, sprawled on the floor, panting and laughing.

Over the years Roosevelt learned even to joke about his condition and boast of his success in combating it. "Maybe my legs aren't so good," he declared gaily, "but look at those shoulders. Jack Dempsey would be green with envy." Even socially, Roosevelt refused to give in. At one dinner party in 1926, his hostess recalled:

He was carried in to a seat at the dining room table. We wondered how he would spend the evening—probably staying in the dining room. But when dinner was over—Franklin pushed back his chair and said—"See me get into the next room." He dropped down on the floor and went in on his hands and knees and got up in another chair by himself.

Through rigorous exercise Roosevelt so perfectly developed his chest, neck, and arm muscles that millions, even in the blinding publicity of the Presidency, were unaware that he was a cripple. His White House aide, Michael Reilly, recalled:

He depended entirely upon his hands and arms and shoulders. Usually, he'd turn his back to the automobile and one of the [Secret Service] Detail would lift him. He'd reach backward until his hands had secured a firm grip on each side of the car door, and then he'd actually surge out of your arms into the car and onto the jump seat. Then he'd reach back once more and

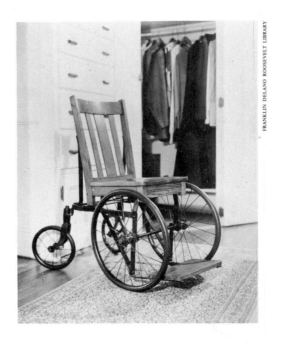

pull himself to the rear seat of the car. He did this with such speed and grace that literally thousands who had seen him at ball games, rallies, and inaugurations never suspected his condition.

Roosevelt's victory over himself was even greater than his triumph over polio. Gone were the old arrogance, the impatience with weakness, the concern with appearances. "If you have spent two years in bed trying to wiggle your big toe," he said, "everything else seems easy." Louis Howe believed that when Roosevelt was flat on his back he "began to see the other fellow's point of view. He thought of others who were ill and afflicted and in want. He dwelt on many things that had not bothered him much before. Lying there, he grew bigger, day by day." "He was serious," Frances Perkins said, "not playing now."

To Eleanor, without whom Roosevelt said he "could never have done

Roosevelt's wheelchair (opposite) was fashioned from a kitchen chair at Hyde Park; he found it easier to get in and out of a chair without arms. Below, in a 1932 photograph, Roosevelt prepares to lift himself out of a car, using only his tremendously powerful arms.

At the 1924 Democratic National Convention, Roosevelt nominated Al Smith for President (left). Although the Governor of New York lost to John Davis, the occasion was a great personal triumph for Roosevelt and marked his re-entry into politics after his polio attack. Above, F.D.R. is shown at Hyde Park during the campaign with (left to right) New York's Lieutenant Governor George Lunn, John Davis, and Al Smith.

it," it seemed that polio "gave him a strength and depth that he did not have as a young man. . . ." She was proud, too, of her husband's victory in still another battle. His mother had pleaded with him to abandon his career—in his son Jimmy's words, to seek "a hole in the good Roosevelt earth at Hyde Park into which he could crawl and hide," to live the life of a pampered invalid, with no responsibilities and no future but the grave. From the outset, F.D.R. would have none of that. He might never play golf again, but he still had his mind, his hands, and a strong heart and he was not about to drop out of the race. Thus "the crippled man who taught a crippled nation to walk," began a new life.

F.D.R. added to his fabulous stamp collection, read naval books, bought the naval prints that still hang in the Hyde Park house. But his life was not sedentary. He accepted a position on the executive committee of the Democratic Party of New York State. He sought publicity by lending his name to several fund-raising campaigns. He urged that a revitalized Democratic Party offer a clear alternative to Republican philosophy and free the American government from the grip of "professional money-makers and to keep it, as was always the intention of our forefathers, in the hands of the people themselves."

Meanwhile, in his private campaign to walk again, Roosevelt had made a heartening discovery. In Vincent Astor's warm, sunlit swimming pool he found that he could move his legs freely, exercising them as he could in no other way. "The water put me where I am," he exulted, "and the water has to bring me back." In December, 1922, he wrote to his old running mate, Cox: "The legs are really coming along finely, and when I am in swimming, work perfectly. This shows that the muscles are all there, only require further strengthening."

If F.D.R.'s hopes for physical recovery were groundless, his political ambitions were not. He carefully tied his political fortunes to those of Alfred E. Smith, elected as New York's governor in 1922 by an unprecedented plurality. At the 1924 Democratic Convention the task of nominating Smith for the Presidency fell to F.D.R., and the occasion was a thundering personal triumph. As Roosevelt, on crutches, made his way painfully to the rostrum, delegates cheered him for three tense, wild minutes. "Franklin looked pale and drawn," writes biographer Allen Churchill. "But on reaching the lectern his face broke into a wide, flashing grin and his head tossed back in the proud old gesture that once annoyed people but now seemed full of gallantry and courage."

In an incisive nominating speech, Roosevelt hailed Smith's "power to strike at error and wrongdoing that makes his adversaries quail before him," and praised "a personality that carries to every hearer not only the sincerity but the righteousness of what he says. He is the 'Happy Warrior' of the political battlefield." For over an hour the ovation continued. The galleries exploded. Delegations demonstrated. It was clear to everyone in the hall that Roosevelt was no less a "happy warrior" than the man he had nominated. A New York *World* editorial spoke for many when it said of F.D.R.: "Adversity has lifted him above the bickering, the religious bigotry, conflicting personal ambitions, and petty sectional prejudices. . . . It has made him the one leader commanding the respect and admiration of delegations from all sections of the land."

Roosevelt also knew that in an era of general prosperity no Democrat would win the Presidency and that even if he became the Democratic candidate, Smith, a Catholic, probably would lose the election on the religious issue alone. Smith, in fact, lost the nomination, but Roosevelt came out of the campaign vastly strengthened as a national political figure.

It would not be unfair to say that this was precisely his intention in backing Smith. Beginning in 1924, he redoubled his efforts to build his own following within the party, cultivating ties with Democratic leaders throughout the country, always careful to deny in public his candidacy for high office while strongly implying it in secret party councils. After the 1924 convention, even Tom Pendergast, the tough Democratic boss of Kansas

Roosevelt first visited the resort at Warm Springs, Georgia, in 1924 (below). He returned often for therapy, swimming, rest, and quiet hours of fishing—sometimes, as at right, with a small captive audience.

UPI

City, could declare: "I want to tell you, that had Mr. Roosevelt . . . been physically able to have withstood the campaign, he would have been named by acclamation. . . . He has the most magnetic personality of any individual I have ever met. . . ."

His job as Smith's campaign manager behind him, Roosevelt returned to his law office, his bonding firm, and his wild business schemes. He began to frequent the Georgia resort of Warm Springs, which had a therapeutic swimming pool fed by buoyant natural mineral waters at a constant

temperature of 88 degrees. From there he happily announced: "I walk around in water 4′ deep without braces or crutches almost as well as if I had nothing the matter with my legs."

Roosevelt's presence attracted other polio victims to the resort's pool. He delighted in teaching his fellow sufferers how to swim, to fight their depression, and to gain new confidence in their powers. Despite F.D.R.'s growing political reputation, his fellow patients' affection for him and their dependence on him was deeply personal. They cherished what one biographer has called "a happy warmth which seemed to be always in him, causing him to talk so often in little wayward jokes, or pour out his energetic laughter. . . ." He bounced about the pool playing ball, or putt-putted around the resort in his special, manually operated Model T, always with a good word for everyone.

Roosevelt so loved the resort that he eventually spent $200,000—two thirds of his fortune—on the property, which he renamed the Georgia Warm Springs Foundation. As President, he made Warm Springs the site

In 1928 the Republican presidential candidate, Herbert Hoover, called himself "a boy from a country village." In a cartoon drawn that year (above), he and his Democratic opponent, New York City boy Al Smith, gallop off to campaign where each knew he was weakest.

of "The Little White House," his summer retreat.

Again in 1928 Governor Smith made a bid for the Presidency. Again Roosevelt nominated him. Again, as he lifted his stricken body up to the speaker's platform, F.D.R. inspired admiration. To a reporter and future historian named Will Durant, he was "a figure tall and proud even in suffering. . . . A man softened and cleansed and illumined with pain." But Smith had a bigger favor to ask.

42

Aware that he had a tough national fight on his hands and that he needed New York to win, Smith begged Roosevelt to run for Governor.

It was a momentous personal decision for F.D.R. He already had taken his first steps unaided and he hoped that if he continued his therapy at Warm Springs he could discard his braces. He knew that the long cold winters in Albany would mean the end of this therapy. He declined Smith's offer. "As I am only forty-six," he wrote in reply, "I feel that I owe it to my family and myself to give the present constant improvement a chance to continue." Smith assured F.D.R. that as Governor of New York he could spend several months a year in Georgia. Roosevelt bluntly replied: "Don't hand me that boloney!"

Smith would not give up. He asked Roosevelt if he would accept the nomination if the Democratic state convention offered it to him, and perhaps sensing Roosevelt's real desire for the post, he encouraged what appears to have been one of the few real "drafts" in American political history. To Eleanor Roosevelt's deep regret, F.D.R. accepted the call.

The campaign was tough, sometimes vicious. Republicans charged that the Democrats had so little hope of victory they had to force the nomination on a cripple. Governor Smith replied that "the Governor does not have to be an acrobat," and that "ninety-nine percent of the work is accomplished at his desk." But that kind of malicious whispering would plague Roosevelt to his death.

If Roosevelt was aware of this mean opposition, he refused to show it. He proved to be a tough campaigner, making as many as sixteen speeches a day while traveling 1,300 miles through New York cities and towns in three weeks. Without such a campaign, it is doubtful that he would have won. As it was, he was elected by an unimpressive margin of 25,564 votes. Smith, caught in the web of anti-Catholic bigotry and national complacency, lost to the Herbert Hoover landslide; he lost even New York state—by over 100,000 votes.

Roosevelt's victory margin was slim, but his personal triumph was great. He had overcome the doubts of his closest advisors, perhaps even his own doubts; he had waged a strenuous campaign, and now he governed the nation's most populous state. Moreover, he was the unchallenged national leader of his party, himself a "happy warrior" on a clear field.

At least during his first term as governor, Roosevelt conducted what one biographer has called "a conspicuously good" if not distinguished administration. He was aware, for example, that not everyone shared in the much-touted prosperity of the times—especially farmers and workingmen. Responding to their needs, he advocated state-administered electrification of farm houses, tax relief for farmers, state-regulated old-age pensions for workers.

On the opposite page, Roosevelt, his wife, and his mother pose before his inauguration as Governor of New York. In a less sedate moment at left, the Governor dons his badge of office as an honorary chieftain of his state's Indians.

Roosevelt encountered opposition on two fronts. Predictably, the Republican-controlled legislature gave him what he happily called "one continuous glorious fight." To Republicans, Roosevelt was a traitor to his class. He was guilty of "avarice" and of blatant "usurpation" of people's rights. Republican opposition was so intense that Roosevelt was forced to defend his budget in court. Perhaps less predictably, Roosevelt was bitterly opposed by former Governor Smith and his allies. The Smith camp was enraged by Roosevelt's success in carrying New York when Smith lost it. Smith also was angered by Roosevelt's refusal to let him continue as

de facto chief executive of the state and by his refusal to reappoint key Smith aides. In a few years Smith would join Roosevelt's bitterest enemies, calling his former friend a dictator and destroyer of the Constitution.

But history would not long permit Roosevelt—or his enemies—the luxury of precinct politics. Less than one year after President Herbert Hoover and Governor Franklin Roosevelt confidently took their oaths of office, America would be plunged into near-revolution. As the tragedy deepened, the nation turned increasingly from the White House to the Executive Mansion in Albany. Franklin Roosevelt's finest hour was approaching.

3

A NEW DEAL FOR AMERICA

On March 4, 1929, President Herbert Hoover ended his cheerful inaugural address by saying: "Ours is a land rich in resources; . . . filled with millions of happy homes; blessed with comfort and opportunity. . . . In no nation are the fruits of accomplishment more secure. . . . I have no fears for the future of our country. It is bright with hope."

America shared Hoover's optimism. In September, 1929, price averages on the New York Stock Exchange were at the highest point in history. General Electric shares, for example, had tripled in value in eighteen months.

To be sure, not everyone had cause for joy. Farmers and factory workers, for example, remained outside the general prosperity they had helped to create. Factories were producing more

As Governor of New York, F.D.R. was exposed to the problems of the Depression. Here, a voter tells Roosevelt his troubles.

goods, but people had less cash to buy them, because wages had not kept pace with high profits. And profits were being used not to build businesses but to speculate wildly in a stock market almost entirely unregulated by law.

Even the stock market reflected a false prosperity. Speculators were "spending" money that they did not have. In the fall of 1929 brokers' loans to investors totaled $8.5 billion, over one half of the entire national debt. Producers of raw materials, such as iron and steel, suffered as the increasing concentration of big business froze prices. Government fiscal policies encouraged inflation, large savings accounts, even the hoarding of gold.

On October 24, 1929, "Black Thursday," the bubble burst. Stock market prices dropped sharply, and panicky investors and brokers went on an incredible selling spree. On that fateful Thursday alone, almost thirteen million shares changed hands at prices that wiped out stockholders,

47

Reginald Marsh's "The Jungle" depicts unemployed New Yorkers during the Depression.

big and small, all over the nation. Despite a brief rally, despite bland assurances by the nation's top bankers that all was well, America's prosperity collapsed in five days.

On "Tragic Tuesday," October 29, nearly sixteen and a half million shares were traded for a total loss of between eight and nine billion dollars. United States Steel, Westinghouse, Montgomery Ward—the giants of American industry—lay prostrate. By mid-November, prices on the New York Stock Exchange had fallen over 40 per cent. Investors' losses were estimated at between twenty-six and thirty billion dollars.

President Hoover assured everyone that the economy was basically sound. All that was needed, he said,

was renewed public confidence in businessmen's good judgment. In January, 1930, Secretary of the Treasury Andrew Mellon calmly declared: "I see nothing in the present situation that is either menacing or warrants pessimism." And in June Hoover announced: "The depression is over."

In fact, however, the stock market crash and the great, nationwide Depression that followed it belied the President's rosy assurances. Between 1929 and 1932 the income of Americans fell from $87.4 billion to a disastrous $41.7 billion. Unemployment soared from four million in 1930 to twelve million in 1932 and sixteen million in March, 1933. In Tennessee, women worked fifty hours a week for $2.39. In Connecticut, girls worked fifty-five hours a week in sweatshop conditions for $1.10 or less.

By the winter of 1932–1933, five thousand banks had failed and nine million savings accounts had been wiped out. Afraid of losing their life savings, people withdrew money from banks, carrying it home in paper bags for safer keeping in mattresses and shoe boxes. Unemployed bond salesmen sold apples on the street. Former clerks knelt on cold sidewalks to shine shoes. Homeless men were glad to be arrested for vagrancy—at least there were warmth and food in jail.

Many unemployed, businessmen and workers alike, committed suicide. While people went hungry, crops rotted in the fields because it was not profitable for farmers to harvest them. Lard replaced butter; families ate stale doughnuts, dandelions, even violet tops. A family that shared a supper of bread dipped in cold milk and sugar was fortunate. People begged from door to door in parts of their neighborhoods where they were not known.

Middle-class Americans, jobless and hungry, swallowed their pride and lined up on the street for handouts of bread and coffee. Homeless men lived in parks night and day. Others, writes historian Arthur Schlesinger, Jr., sought warmth and shelter, "huddled together in doorways, in empty packing cases, in boxcars," even resting on piles of refuse near municipal incinerators. Miners and their families in West Virginia and Kentucky, evicted from their homes because they could not pay the rent, were forced to move into flimsy tents during the winter.

From New York City's Central Park to St. Louis and Portland, Oregon, makeshift "cities" of tarpaper shacks sprang up and were named "Hoovervilles" after the President who had failed to act. People stuffed cardboard into their shoes, and newspapers beneath their shirts, to keep out the cold. Schools closed, as malnutrition struck down pupils and teachers. Workers lucky enough to find jobs soon were limited to two or three days a week. Farmers, their income cut by two-thirds between 1929 and 1932, were unable to pay rent or taxes and thus lost their houses and their land.

America was on the verge of revolution. In Nebraska, Minnesota, and Iowa, normally conservative farmers declared a "farm holiday," determined to withhold their produce from the cities unless they got a fair price. Milk was dumped on highways, sheep perished in mass slaughters, roads were blockaded. Starving miners in Virginia smashed grocery store windows for food. In March, 1932, three thousand jobless workers, marching —with police permission—to demand justice at the Ford auto plant at Dearborn, Michigan, were repulsed with tear gas and machine-gun fire; four died. That same year several thousand World War I veterans marched on Capitol Hill to beg Congress for early payment of the bonus promised them

TEXT CONTINUED ON PAGE 53

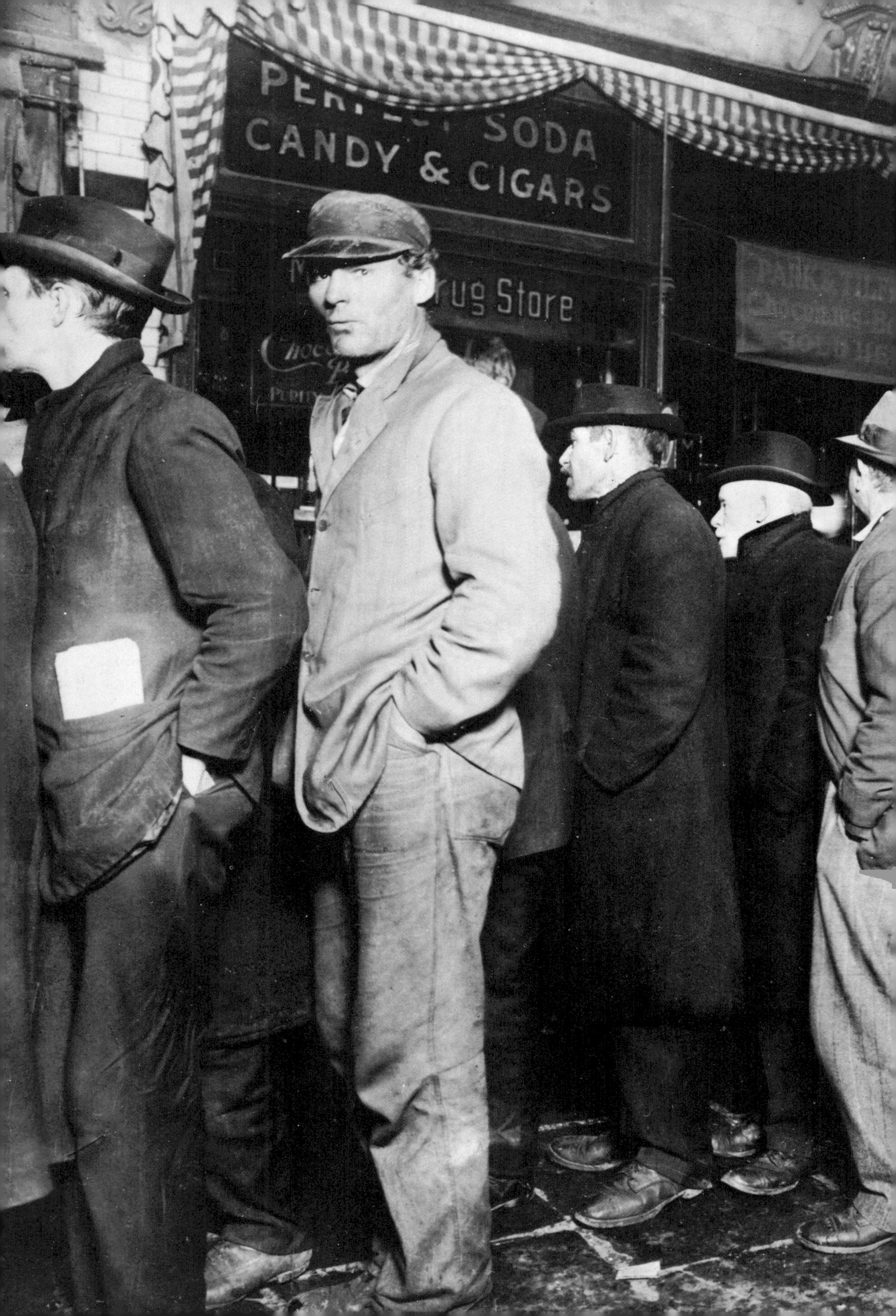
CANDY & CIGARS
Store

THE POVERTY OF
THE DEPRESSION

When F.D.R. was named President in 1932, twelve million people—one quarter of the nation's work force—were unemployed. Realizing that local authorities were powerless to relieve such widespread poverty, Roosevelt charged the U.S. government with much of that obligation, as Hoover never had been willing to do.

The Depression meant bread lines in the cities and starvation wages on the farms.

51

When disgruntled veterans of World War I came to Washington in 1932 to seek the early payment of a promised war bonus, they lived in an improvised tent city. Congress failed to authorize their bonus, and Hoover, refusing to see them, ordered their pathetic shantytown burned.

TEXT CONTINUED FROM PAGE 49

for 1945. On orders from the Hoover administration, their squalid huts were put to the torch. Soldiers with fixed bayonets and tanks, led by General Douglas MacArthur and Major Dwight D. Eisenhower, drove the veterans and their families out of Washington. Said the *Washington News:* "What a pitiful spectacle is that of the great American Government, mightiest in the world, chasing unarmed men, women and children with Army tanks. ... If the Army must be called out to make war on unarmed citizens, this is no longer America."

President Hoover, who had refused to talk to the veterans, opposed federal action to aid victims of the Depression. He rejected proposed public works programs to put people to work, and even low-cost housing, because he felt that such measures struck at "the roots of self-government." The Depression, he announced, was a local problem; people must "fight their own battles in their own communities."

He was unmoved by the fact that America's cities and towns were bankrupt and that by 1932 only one quarter of the jobless got any relief at all. He rejected even an industry-proposed business planning council as "sheer fascism." He remained convinced that "the sole function of government is to bring about a condition of affairs favorable to the beneficial development of private enterprise." If businessmen recovered, he reasoned, workers and farmers would prosper as well.

Governor Roosevelt begged to differ. In March, 1930, he described the Depression for what it was: "The situation is serious, and the time has come for us to face this unpleasant fact dispassionately and constructively as a scientist faces a test tube of deadly germs. ...." America's economy was sick; a cure must be found. One cause of its illness, he said in April, was the concentration of wealth in a few hands, with the consequence that buying power was unevenly distributed. These were bold words, and increasingly, Democratic leaders looked to the Governor of New York as their logical candidate for President in 1932.

When Hoover sent leading Cabinet members to speak against Roosevelt in his bid for re-election as Governor in 1930, Roosevelt tore into them. Winding up his campaign at Carnegie Hall, Roosevelt condemned the Republicans for failing to fight the Depression: "I say to these gentlemen:" he declared, "We shall be grateful if you will return to your posts in Washington, and bend your efforts and spend your time solving the problems which the whole nation is [bearing] under your administration." New York, he said, could take care of itself without federal interference.

The voters responded with hope, and re-elected Roosevelt by a stunning margin of 725,001 votes. He took 41 out of the 57 counties outside of New York City, winning easily even in Republican upstate New York by a large plurality.

As a young attorney, Roosevelt had told a friend: "Anyone who is governor of New York has a good chance to be president with any luck." And Governor Roosevelt, at the beginning of his second term, was off and running for the big prize. His political troubleshooter, James A. Farley, his speechwriter, Judge Samuel Rosenman, Louis Howe, and others now began laying the groundwork for his national campaign. The Governor's actions and speeches were carefully weighted so that all the American people could see that there was an alternative to Hooverism. New York would be the laboratory of reform, of bold leadership in fighting the Depression. It would be made clear that what New York could do the nation could do—and do it best under F.D.R.

As early as June, 1930, Roosevelt had advocated unemployment insurance, the first prominent American politician to do so. Before his re-election, also, he had a national reputation as an advocate of regional farm planning, conservation, and government regulation of power companies. "If we in the United States virtually give up the control over the utilities of the nation," he had said in 1929, "attacks on other liberties will follow."

Armed with a mandate of almost three quarters of a million votes, F.D.R. began his second term as Governor by attacking those who insisted that despite the Depression, government had no right to "intervene" in the economy on behalf of people hungry and jobless through no fault of their own. He was angered by "expert" suggestions that the Depression, in obedience to unnamed economic laws, must run its course while decent people begged for food, lost their savings, and lived in shacks. "People aren't cattle, you know!" he told one such orthodox economist.

On August 28, 1931, Roosevelt addressed a special session of the New York legislature. The cave man, he said, in a now classic speech, fought alone and unprotected for his day-to-day survival in a hostile world. But civilization had changed all that. Men had learned to co-operate. Men had established governments to serve and protect people. Most particularly, he explained, the state was "the duly constituted representative of an organized society of human beings, created by them for their mutual well-being."

Government, Roosevelt declared, was not an impersonal, abstract force; it existed not to dictate but to serve. It must fulfill "the duty of the servant to its master." This was government's only justification for being. Most especially, Roosevelt said, the government must care "for those of its citizens who find themselves the victims of such adverse circumstance as makes them unable to obtain even the necessities for mere existence without the aid of others." When there were no jobs for the jobless, Roosevelt said, the government was obliged to help financially, "not as a matter of charity, but as a matter of social duty."

54

Roosevelt knew that New York's cities and towns were bankrupt. He therefore asked for and won a state-administered Temporary Emergency Relief Administration—the first of its kind in the United States. Its $20 million fund (later greatly increased) was to be financed by a 50 per cent increase in the state income tax. In six years it would bring Depression relief to 40 per cent of the state's population.

Roosevelt also created jobs on public works projects, including conservation, reforestation, and land reclamation. He fought for improved working conditions, relief to farmers threatened by mortgage foreclosures, and unsuccessfully, for unemployment insurance. "We are in a new era to which I do not belong . . ." former President Calvin Coolidge would declare in 1932. "These new ideas call for new men to develop them. That task is not for men who believe in the only kind of government I know anything about." Roosevelt was one of

In 1930 Roosevelt was elected Governor of New York for the second time. Yet at Warm Springs he was his own man, driving around the countryside, treeing possum if the mood struck him.

THE ADMIRAL SHIPS A CREW　☆☆☆　BY ARGENS

Editorial

Hoover or Hearst?

A 1932 cartoon shows three candidates for the Democratic presidential nomination—F.D.R., Garner, and William McAdoo—seeking the support of newspaper publisher William R. Hearst.

the new men. "It is time we experimented . . . ," he declared in 1931. "Please do not dismiss these ideas with the word radical. Remember the radical of yesterday is almost [always] the reactionary of today."

Campaigning for the presidential nomination, Roosevelt enlarged his "Brain Trust," or circle of advisors, to include such political and economic experts as professors Raymond Moley and Rexford Tugwell of Columbia. On the road, Jim Farley lined up convention delegates by playing on

Roosevelt's famous name and bold new leadership in Albany. When the Democratic National Convention opened in Chicago in June, 1932, Roosevelt already had $666\frac{1}{4}$ of the 770 votes needed for the presidential nomination.

In securing these votes, Roosevelt played politics as ruthlessly as any big city boss before him. As the political slogan goes, he "carried water on both shoulders"; he had something for everyone, as long as he had their votes. To gain the support of William

Randolph Hearst's powerful newspaper chain, for example, he denounced the League of Nations—the dream of his old patron and mentor, Woodrow Wilson. Despite his own state public works projects, Roosevelt derided Al Smith's proposal for similar programs on a national scale. Smith's plan, F.D.R. said, dealt with the "symptoms" rather than the "bacteria" in the economic system.

On the other hand, with no evident awareness of the contradiction, F.D.R. insisted that the federal government must cease to be a spectator and come to the aid of "the forgotten man at the bottom of the economic pyramid." He assailed big business, particularly what he called "that small group of men whose chief outlook upon the social welfare is tinctured by the fact that they can make huge profits. . . ." He urged new approaches to the economic crisis. "The country needs . . . , the country demands bold, persistent experimentation, . . ." he declared. "Above all, try something. . . . The millions who are in want will not stand silently by forever while the things to satisfy their needs are within easy reach."

These were heady words, not only for Republicans but also for old-line backroom politicians and conservative Democrats like Al Smith. Some might dismiss F.D.R. as "another Hoover," as a vacillating lightweight whose only principle was to gain power. But Smith and his lieutenants, still smarting over their defeat in 1928, were worried. Roosevelt had proved in Albany that he could not be bossed. What reason was there to believe that he would even consult loyal party regulars if he went to Washington? Besides, what if he really believed all this pie-in-the-sky idealism that his professors were feeding him? In a blistering address, Smith denounced Roosevelt for "setting class against class," thus preparing the way for revolution.

The battle shifted to the convention floor. On the third ballot, Roosevelt had increased his lead only to 682 votes, with 770 needed to win. The pros were alarmed by the threat of a stalemate and of another internal party war. Farley swung into action. Assured that its favorite son, John Nance Garner, would be selected as Vice-President, Texas came out for Roosevelt, and so, too, did California, which had been pledged to Garner. On the fourth ballot, Roosevelt polled 945 votes to Smith's 190. The band struck up what was to become F.D.R.'s familiar campaign song, "Happy Days Are Here Again."

Traditionally, presidential nominees had waited in feigned ignorance until they were told officially of their victory. Roosevelt knew that he had won and saw no reason to pretend that he did not. The campaign for the White House would begin immediately. Accompanied by Eleanor, his sons John and Elliott, his staff and his bodyguards, Roosevelt boarded a frail three-engined plane in Albany. He would fly to Chicago and accept the nomination in person at the convention. Informed of Roosevelt's decision, the delegates tuned in to radio reports of his progress. His plane was buffeted by winds. It was forced to refuel. It was delayed repeatedly. But the flight itself was a bold political stroke. "... His decision to fly," writes Frank Freidel, "was something of a novelty in a period when commercial air transport was still in its infancy. To a country stagnating in depression, Roosevelt's bold dramatic action brought a lift of hope."

At Chicago Stadium, where he was to deliver his address, Roosevelt was applauded wildly. Over their radios Americans heard his crisp, reassuring voice denouncing "wild radicalism"; calling for "an orderly and hopeful spirit on the part of the millions of our people who have suffered so much." He assured his listeners that the old order had passed, that the old injustices must end. In words that electrified the nation, F.D.R. made a solemn promise:

I pledge you, I pledge myself, to a new deal for the American people. Let us all here assembled constitute ourselves prophets of a new order of competence and of courage. This is more than a political campaign; it is a call to arms. Give me your help, not to win votes alone, but to win in this crusade to restore America to its own people.

TEXT CONTINUED ON PAGE 62

Abolition of the bread lines and repeal of Prohibition were two planks in the 1932 Democratic platform, espoused by presidential candidate Roosevelt and his running mate, John Nance Garner. The license plate above drew the thirsty; signs like that below rallied the hungry.

THE CHARISMATIC CAMPAIGNER

When Roosevelt addressed an audience while on campaign, something like an electric charge passed between them, stimulating each to greater confidence in the other. He planned his itineraries with the greatest care, delivering a major speech every few days, and ad-libbing frequent informal talks on precisely the regional issue that would make his listeners come alive. Careful preparation and a prodigious memory helped, but only so great a gift for politics could make politics look so easy.

During the 1932 campaign Roosevelt traveled 27,000 miles, many of them in "The Roosevelt Special." At every stop he would appear on the observation platform of the last car (above) with members of his family, say a few words, and be exhilarated by seeing his smile reflected in the faces of his listeners. Below, Roosevelt carries the search for votes to Georgia.

In the 1932 election Roosevelt made his weakest showing in New England. Above, he manfully wolfs a sandwich during one of several campaign visits to Massachusetts, a state he nevertheless carried by only a narrow margin. That December the residents of Warm Springs, below, crowded around Roosevelt's automobile, eager to shake the hand of their next President.

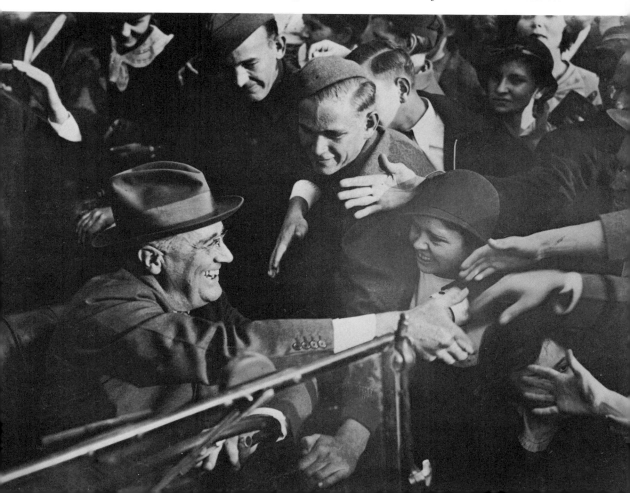

TEXT CONTINUED FROM PAGE 58

As the promise was fulfilled, his words were remembered and the domestic policies of his administrations became known as the New Deal.

Not everyone shared the convention's enthusiasm for Roosevelt. New Jersey's Democratic boss, Frank Hague, predicted that he wouldn't carry a single state west of the Mississippi. A leading magazine of the time derided F.D.R. as "God's greatest gift to the Republican Party." The political columnist Walter Lippmann had dismissed him as "a pleasant man, who, without any important qualifications for the office, would like very much to be President."

Most Democrats, however, were confident from the start that Roosevelt would win easily. They urged their candidate to wage a leisurely "front-porch" campaign, to avoid excessive traveling, to make extensive use of the radio, which Roosevelt was indeed to master as an instrument of public persuasion. John Garner, F.D.R.'s running mate, assured him: "All you have to do is to stay alive until election day." Hoover, convinced that Roosevelt would lose the confidence of Eastern businessmen and therefore forfeit the election, calmly planned to make only three or four speeches in his campaign for re-election.

Once again, Roosevelt's opponents misjudged him. F.D.R. wore out the aides and newsmen who accompanied him on his 27,000-mile, coast-to-coast campaign. From the rear platform of "The Roosevelt Special," his campaign train, Roosevelt carried a message of hope and reform to city after city, town after town. In firm, simple terms he spoke to jobless workers in Kansas and New York, Missouri and Oregon. Leaning on his cane or on the arm of his son, he stood erect and talked with coal miners and farmers, asking questions, giving them confidence in the future. They gave him confidence, too, and a new belief in the rightness of his cause. He felt and he voiced their anger, their desire for change. And in their poverty and fear, they moved him deeply: "I have looked into the faces of thousands of Americans . . ." he said. "They have the frightened look of lost children."

But Frances Perkins had been right. Roosevelt was no tub-thumping radical. He was at once the product and the spokesman of the capitalist order. Not once did he question the basic rightness of that order. And in his speeches promising to correct its injustices there was, in general, little to indicate that he intended to move it to the left or right. For example, he promised federal relief to the jobless with one breath and a cut in federal spending with another. He advocated free international trade, and at the same time, insisted on high tariffs to protect American industries.

A program of national relief comparable to that of New York State clearly would require deficit spending, at least initially. But as piously as a good Republican, Roosevelt called for a balanced budget. To put it charitably, the future architect of the New Deal and its barrelful of federal agencies was less than honest in accusing poor Herbert Hoover of financial extravagance. Hoover, Roosevelt declared, had rashly adopted the idea that "we ought to center control of everything in Washington as rapidly as possible." Yet the next moment Roosevelt himself was promising federal regulation of the stock market, aid to farmers in fighting mortgage foreclosures, federal programs of old-age benefits and unemployment insurance. In short, like a true politician, he told his audiences what they wanted to hear, because he wanted their votes.

Only in a speech at the Commonwealth Club in San Francisco on September 23 did Roosevelt map the philosophy of the future New Deal. The first priorities, he said then, were a fairer distribution of wealth, greater purchasing power among the people, and equal job opportunities. As in Albany, he demanded that America begin "adapting existing economic organizations to the service of the people." He assailed the "some 600-odd corporations [that] . . . controlled two thirds of American industry" and predicted an "economic oligarchy" if big corporations were not made to behave. As eloquently as any progressive before him, or since, he declared: "I do not believe that in the name of that sacred word individualism, a few powerful interests should be permitted to make industrial cannon fodder of

the lives of half the population of the United States."

Herbert Hoover, alarmed by Roosevelt's growing popularity with the crowds, began to campaign more vigorously. The President declared that Roosevelt was "proposing changes and so-called new deals which would destroy the very foundations of our American system"; that he had embraced "a philosophy of government which has poisoned all Europe," including Stalin's Russia. A Democratic victory, Hoover told a nation with fourteen million unemployed, would mean that "grass will grow in the streets of a hundred cities" and "bring disaster to every fireside in America." Roosevelt replied briefly and angrily: "I simply will not let Hoover question my Americanism."

As election day neared, Hoover panicked. This gentle man, who had served in the White House without pay, who had supervised the feeding of hungry Europeans after World War I, persuaded himself that his re-election meant the salvation of capitalism and freedom. "Thank God," he said, "we still have a government in Washington that knows how to deal with the mob." But Roosevelt, himself rich, himself a member of the ruling class, was keenly aware that unless "the mob" was somehow fed and put to work, America would face revolution.

The conservative press might attack Roosevelt as a madman and a rabble-rousing Red, but if F.D.R. was

hurt, he did not show it. He had a message of hope for the American people, a plan, he said, to help them. And on election day, 1932, it became clear that the message had gotten through. Roosevelt triumphed with 22,809,638 votes to Hoover's 15,758,901. He carried all but six states. In the Electoral College he won by 472 to 59. It was the greatest vote of confidence that had ever been given to an American President.

In the four months between the election and the inauguration, unemployment rose even higher. More banks failed. Although Hoover's inaction and tragically unsound fiscal policies were major factors, Hoover blamed the deepening Depression on Roosevelt, alleging that businessmen were afraid of him. To embarrass the President-elect, Hoover urged him publicly to join him in a formal declaration of policy, which, by Hoover's own admission, would commit F.D.R. in advance to "the abandonment of 90% of the so-called new deal." Armed with a genuine mandate for change, Roosevelt refused. Until March 4, 1933, Roosevelt said, it would be both improper and unwise for him to participate in government decisions.

On February 15, 1933, cruising off the Florida coast with his friend Vincent Astor, the President-elect stopped off in Miami. At a bayfront park he

In February, 1933, in Miami, Anton Cermak, Chicago's Mayor, was fatally wounded by an assassin who meant to kill Roosevelt.

addressed a meeting of the American Legion. "As Father finished his brief remarks," his son James recalled, "five shots were heard," aimed directly at the Presidential party. They came from an eight-dollar revolver belonging to Giuseppe Zangara, an unemployed bricklayer crazed by an intense hatred for "all officials and everybody who is rich."

Five of the Presidential party were hit, Mayor Anton Cermak of Chicago fatally. The police closed in, Vincent Astor recalled, kneeling on Zangara "to hide him from the view of the crowd, which might have lynched him." Had Roosevelt been shot? The crowd panicked. No! From the limousine came his reassuring, powerful voice: "I'm all right! I'm all right!" Then the President-elect drove to a hospital with the dying Cermak in his arms. Cermak turned to the new President, said "I'm mighty glad it was me instead of you," and died. Shocked Americans gained new respect for the sheer physical courage of the man they had chosen to lead them.

On Inauguration Day, March 4, 1933, Roosevelt rode to the Capitol steps to take his oath of office. Hoover sat at his side in silence, despite the cheers of the crowd. As the limousine moved along Pennsylvania Avenue, F.D.R. remained silent, too, out of respect for the retiring President. The cheers continued and Roosevelt lost patience. "I said to myself, 'Spinach!'" he recalled. "'Protocol or no protocol, somebody has to do something.' The two of us simply couldn't sit there on our hands, ignoring each other and everyone else. So I began to wave my own response with my top hat and I kept waving it until I got to the inauguration stand and was sworn in."

At that stand, his hand on the family Bible, Franklin Delano Roosevelt took his oath of office as the thirty-second President of the United States. From coast to coast, the nation listened to its radios. What would happen to America? Where were they going? In a speech that ranks with the finest in inaugural oratory, the new President answered their questions: "This great nation will endure as it has endured, will revive and will prosper."

Then Roosevelt uttered the words for which he is best remembered: "So, first of all, let me assert my firm belief that the only thing we have to fear is fear itself,—nameless, unreasoning, unjustified terror which paralyzes needed efforts to convert retreat into advance." There was no reason for hunger and unemployment in a nation so much blessed with mighty businesses and rich natural resources. Depression had come, Roosevelt declared, through the bungling of a handful of men who could see no further than their pocketbooks. But now their day was over. Now, he said, America had asked for change and it would get change. "The money changers have fled from their high seats in the temple of our civilization." The people once more were re-established

as masters of their government.

"Our greatest primary task," President Roosevelt said, "is to put people to work." To do this, America needed "a disciplined attack upon our common problems," deliberate planning by the "great army of our people." As the leader of this attack, Roosevelt promised, he would try to preserve America's traditional balance of executive and legislative authority. But, he warned, if this traditional balance proved unequal to the task of ending the Depression, he would ask Congress for no less than emergency powers, "as great," he said, "as the power that would be given to me if we were in fact invaded by a foreign foe." Hunger, unemployment, and fear, by some means, would be conquered. The people had chosen him to lead that conquest. "In the spirit of the gift," the President said, "I take it."

Then began the famous "First Hundred Days" of the Roosevelt Administration. First he closed the banks to prevent the mass withdrawals that were ruining them. Next he called Congress into special session, to ask for, and receive, overwhelming bipartisan support for a series of reforms without precedent in American history.

An Emergency Banking Relief Act enabled banks to reopen their doors nine days after Roosevelt took office. The Treasury was authorized to issue new currency, to give the people the buying power that they badly needed. Within two weeks of Roosevelt's tak-

Inaugural Address —

I am certain that my fellow Americans expect that
on my induction into the Presidency I will address them
with a candor and a decision which the present situation
of our nation impels.   This is preeminently the time
to speak the truth, the whole truth, frankly and boldly.
Nor need we shrink from being honest *by being* as to the condition
of our country today.   This great nation will endure
as it has endured, will revive and will prosper.   So
first of all let me assert my firm belief that the only
thing we have to fear is fear itself, - nameless, unreasoning,
unjustified terror which paralyzes ~~the needed~~ *needed* efforts *to*
convert retreat into advance.
~~to bring about prosperity once more.~~

~~In the crisis of our War for Independence; in the~~
~~poverty, the unrest and the doubts of the early days~~
~~of our constitutional government;~~ later in the dark days
~~of the war between the states,~~ a leadership of frankness
and vigor, met with that understanding and support of
the people themselves which is essential to victory.
I am convinced that you will again give that support to

Roosevelt's copy of his first inaugural address shows how carefully he edited his speeches.

67

ing office the stock market averages had risen some fifteen per cent.

When Roosevelt took the United States off the gold standard, the banking house of Morgan declared that his action "saved the country from complete collapse." With bills now payable in silver or paper money, with more money in circulation, prices and stocks rose. Consumer buying power increased, and business prospered.

Through the Civilian Conservation Corps, authorized in the First Hundred Days, two and a half million men eventually would be put to work. They would build dams, plant forests, fight soil erosion, and build state and national parks that still flourish.

Five billion dollars in direct relief would go to cities and states, under the Federal Emergency Relief Act, originally passed in May.

The Emergency Farm Mortgage Act halted foreclosures; mortgages were refunded with federal money. Under the Agricultural Adjustment Act, farm prices were guaranteed, as they are now, through crop curtail-

Before Roosevelt established the Tennessee Valley Authority, erosion had carved a moonscape in the valley's floor (below). The TVA's 480-foot-high Fontana Dam, opposite, is the highest of more than twenty-five dams providing hydroelectric power and irrigation to the valley. The system has made the Tennessee River navigable for 650 miles, from Knoxville to the Ohio River.

ment, planned use of land, and parity payments. The new Farm Credit Administration reduced interest rates on farm loans and made new ones.

Forty thousand square miles in the Tennessee Valley Basin were saved by the Tennessee Valley Authority. This pioneer agency, administered by the government because no private firm could afford it, harnessed the Tennessee River. In so doing, it provided cheap electricity to homes, farms, and factories. It assured soil conservation, flood control, irrigation, and an in-

dustrial boom. It was to be a model for nations all over the world.

The kind of wild stock speculation that had ruined the country in 1929 was minimized by the Truth-in-Securities Act. This law protected investors by requiring brokers to file sworn information regarding their securities with the Federal Trade Commission.

Nonfarm homeowners in danger of losing their houses were allowed to refinance their mortgages at more reasonable interest rates, through the newly created Home Owners Loan

Corporation. They also were able to borrow money more easily for taxes and repairs. One in five Americans could thank HOLC for his home.

Savings accounts, which had been wiped out by the stock market crash and the bank failures, now were protected against loss by a newly created agency named the Federal Deposit Insurance Corporation.

The National Industrial Recovery Act required businesses to abide by fair practices in competition and merchandising. This law also gave labor unions the right to organize and bargain with management for their rights. The famous Public Works Administration, created by the Recovery Act, provided still more construction jobs for the millions of unemployed.

Only a month after his inauguration, cartoonists were saluting Roosevelt's enormous energy.

Although big businessmen benefited as much as workers and farmers from the reforms of the First Hundred Days, they scoffed at F.D.R.'s program. But workers who had stood in the bread lines and now had jobs, and farmers who now were guaranteed a fair return on their crops, rejoiced.

It is true that Roosevelt did not "end" the Depression. As late as 1940, seven and a half million Americans still were unemployed, and only the booming economy of World War II truly ended the Depression. But Roosevelt did cut unemployment, and he restored confidence in business and in the government itself, thereby averting almost certain revolution. Moreover, he accomplished these goals not by becoming the kind of dictator to which much of Europe had turned in its desperation, but by channeling major reforms through established economic and political structures. For this achievement, Roosevelt was despised not only by die-hard conservatives but also by radicals of the Left and Right. As one loyal spokesman for the old order put it: "Well, anyway, this fellow Roosevelt may not be sound, but he has certainly taken the wind out of the radicals' sails."

In tackling the problems of the Depression, Roosevelt the President, like Roosevelt the Governor, was guided by the general conviction that government had a duty to serve people and help them through crises beyond their control. To be sure, well-fed industrialists muttered about "Bolshevism" and "fascism" over cocktails in fashionable clubs and delighted in condemning "that man in the White House." But the New Deal, in the words of Samuel Eliot Morison, was in fact "American as a bale of hay . . . a new deal of old cards no longer stacked against the common man" that "probably . . . saved the capitalist system in the United States. . . ."

"It is common sense," Roosevelt said, "to take a method and try it. If it fails, admit it frankly and try another." Certainly, no single "ism," no master scheme, governed Roosevelt's experiments. "To look upon these policies as the result of a unified plan," wrote Roosevelt's "brain-truster" Raymond Moley, "was to believe that the accumulation of stuffed snakes, baseball pictures, school flags, old tennis shoes, carpenter's tools, geometry books, and chemistry sets in a boy's bedroom could have been put there by an interior decorator."

But there can be no doubt of Roosevelt's capacity to restore Americans' faith in themselves and their institutions. Under his leadership, as William Leuchtenburg points out, Congress wrote into law "the most extraordinary series of reforms in the nation's history." Republican Senator Hiram Johnson of California said of the new President: "The admirable trait in Roosevelt is that he has the guts to try. . . . Where there was hesitation . . . feebleness, timidity, . . . there are now courage and boldness and real action."

4

"THAT MAN IN THE WHITE HOUSE"

"The Republican National Committee," Roosevelt once said in high good humor, was "proclaiming from housetops that the Democratic Party wished A. To amend the Ten Commandments B. To add to the Ten Commandments C. To scrap the Ten Commandments. On this issue," the President added, "they are confident that they can sweep the country."

F.D.R. was, in fact, quoting a Senate humorist. But these sentiments were not uncommon, especially in wealthy and conservative circles, as Roosevelt pushed forward with the New Deal. Most of what F.D.R. and the Congress did to curb the Depression—in the First Hundred Days and afterward—has been embodied in government institutions that are now as much a part of the American tradition as the Lincoln Memorial. Social Security, minimum wage laws, soil

Roosevelt was clearly exhilarated, not worn down, by the challenges of his second term.

conservation and housing programs—it would be difficult to imagine American life without them.

In the 1930's, however, Roosevelt's schemes seemed revolutionary to conservative businessmen. Accustomed to neutrality at the least—and sometimes outright favoritism—from the White House, big business fumed as Congress churned out reform after reform, "like candy bars popping out of a slot machine."

One liberal insisted that "the New Deal is simply the effort of a lot of half-baked Socialists to save capitalism for the dumb capitalists." The United States Communist Party boss, Earl Browder, condemned Roosevelt for turning the public treasury into "a huge trough where the big capitalists eat their fill." Other radicals angrily charged that Roosevelt, in a series of cunning deceptions, had emasculated the revolution and saved the system that had made him rich.

But a lot of old-timers saw it another way. In the view of one enraged judge, Roosevelt was "playing tiddly-winks with the entire universe." Others assailed him as "King Franklin," a grinning autocrat, "that Red in the White House," a prestigious front man for conspiratorial racial and religious minorities out to destroy White, Anglo-Saxon, Protestant America.

Roosevelt was himself an expert at the political curve ball, and he took such attacks as part of the game. Besides, as one close aide put it, he was well aware that his personality and policies "so divided people that those who loved him will hear no evil, and those who hated him will tolerate no praise."

Like Jefferson, like Jackson, like his cousin Teddy Roosevelt, F.D.R. loved power and loved politics. Like Teddy, he might insist grandly: "I have read history and known presidents; it's a terrible job. But somebody has to do it." But the fact is, as his secretary Grace Tully recalled, that from the moment he entered the White House, Roosevelt was impelled by "a *will* to assume primary responsibility for events." He was "the Boss," as the White House staff called him. He was the commander in chief. And in the exercise of his constitutional functions he used every means of persuasion, communication, and control available to him.

He was the first President, for example, to realize the awesome influence of the White House press conference. He held them regularly in his office, and they were freewheeling, give-and-take sessions. Reporters, with whom he was often on a first-name basis, loved him. He was "good copy," and he didn't stand on his dignity. "Will reporters be allowed to use the new swimming pool and play tennis on the White House courts?" one newsman asked him. "Of course," the President replied, "and the children have a sandpile. You boys can play in it, if you like."

More than a decade before television, radio made Roosevelt's voice familiar in the kitchens and living rooms of millions of American farms and homes. In his famous "fireside chats," broadcast over all the major networks, Roosevelt explained the problems that he and the nation were facing. With elegant simplicity he outlined his plans to solve these problems and asked for the people's help and trust. Public response was phenomenal. Roosevelt reached people. They felt, for the most part, that he was "their" President, and that despite his crisp Eastern accent, he was not talking down to them. They felt that he cared for them. "Dear Mr. President:" a grateful homeowner wrote, "This is just to tell you that everything is all right now. The man you sent found our house all right, and we went down to the bank with him and the mortgage can go on for a while longer. You remember I wrote you about losing the furniture too. Well, your man got it back for us. . . ."

In the drab Depression years the White House itself became a focus of

"MOTHER, WILFRED WROTE A BAD WORD!"

Roosevelt's whirlwind program of social reform extended the power of the government largely to benefit the people impoverished by the Depression. As the nation's cartoonists were quick to note, this policy did not please the rich, many of whom considered F.D.R. a traitor to his class. The "Oath of Allegiance" is one of the milder jibes at Roosevelt's autocratic optimism.

PROPOSED OATH OF ALLEGIANCE TO THE DEMOCRATIC PARTY

I pledge allegiance to the Democratic Party, and to the Roosevelt Family for which it stands, One Family Indespensable — with divorces and Captaincies for all.

Four thousand years ago Moses said to his people: "Pick up your shovels, mount your asses, load your camels, and ride to the Promised Land".

Four thousand years later Mr. Roosevelt said to HIS people, "Throw down your shovels, sit on your asses, light a Camel: THIS IS the Promised Land.

SIGN HERE_____

FRANKLIN DELANO ROOSEVELT LIBRARY

75

Roosevelt's witty and well-phrased responses made him a favorite with journalists. At Hyde Park the President's news conferences often were al fresco affairs like the one above.

color and glamour, as celebrated movie actresses, authors, and artists dined with the President. Like few presidents before him, F.D.R. had a sure instinct for the dramatic gesture. He became a familiar and impressive figure in his velvet-collared, coat-length, black Navy cape, moving with an air of "vibrant aliveness," breathing confidence, his cigarette holder clamped cockily between his teeth. He knew the words for "my old friend" in eleven languages and slapped backs with the best of them. Members of racial and religious minorities—held pretty much at arm's length by previous presidents—were welcome at the White House, as were small businessmen, labor union leaders, intellectuals. Women found a new champion in Eleanor Roosevelt, who roamed the country on fact-finding good-will tours for her husband, and in Secretary of Labor Frances Perkins, the nation's first woman Cabinet member.

Life in the White House—or at Hyde Park—seemed brighter when the First Family, several generations strong, gathered to light the national Christmas tree or for Thanksgiving dinner. All over the White House F.D.R.'s booming, jaunty voice could be heard, often in good-natured teasing. His solemn Secretary of the Treasury, Henry Morgenthau, Jr., an old friend, was "Henry the Morgue." His speechwriter and confidant, Judge Samuel Rosenman, was "Sammy the Rose."

F.D.R. delighted, too, in bursting

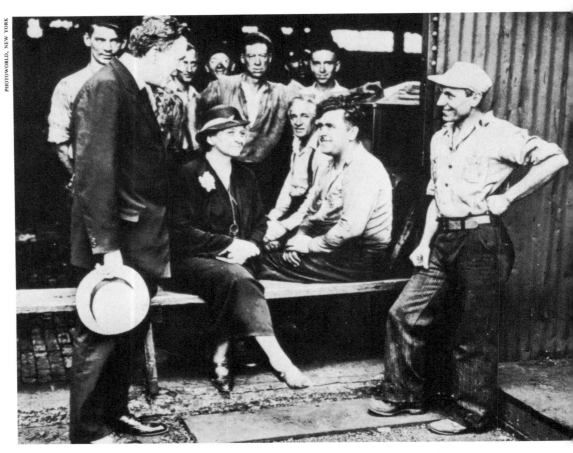

Frances Perkins was Secretary of Labor during Roosevelt's entire term as President. In the early days, above, she traveled extensively, checking the effectiveness of New Deal programs.

old balloons. He was proud of his own Dutch ancestry, but at least publicly he opposed the notion that early arrival in the United States gave any group of Americans a special claim to patriotism. He announced to a shocked convention of the Daughters of the American Revolution: "You and I . . . are descended from immigrants and revolutionists." Not even royalty awed him. When King George VI and his queen, Elizabeth, visited Hyde Park—the first reigning British monarchs to visit the United States—

they were treated to hot dogs. At 1:30 A.M., after one convivial evening, F.D.R. informed the King: "Young man, it's time for you to go to bed."

For relaxation President Roosevelt worked with his already formidable stamp collection. He now enjoyed a special privilege: he put the State Department on notice to send him a sack of foreign stamps every week. He found escape, too, in his swimming pool, in lively poker games, or in going yachting with those millionaires who still remained his friends.

Ironically, while F.D.R. never hesitated to commit the federal government to vast spending programs, and was an extravagant collector of stamps and old sailing prints, he was otherwise something of a tightwad. He wore his own jackets—and his sons' castoffs—into the ground. His felt campaign hat, which he thought brought him good luck, would not have appealed to a hobo. And as his son Jimmy recalls, he liked to boast that he sliced turkey so thin you could "almost *read* through it!"

One White House aide, Raymond Moley, was alarmed by F.D.R.'s "frightening" openness to ideas. "So far as I know," Moley once said, "he makes no effort to check up on anything that I or anyone else has told him." But the same observer conceded that in the clinch Roosevelt acted alone. "When he wants something a lot he can be formidable—when crossed he is hard, stubborn, resourceful, relentless." He excelled in the fine political art of "divide and conquer," cunningly pitting one man's ambition against another's. Often he assigned the same task to different aides without telling any of them that others were involved.

Like presidents before and after him, Roosevelt knew the value of political window-dressing and the appearance, at least, of nonpartisanship. He would, for instance, name Republican Henry L. Stimson as his Secretary of War. And to the conservative Texan Jesse Jones, who was well to the right of center, F.D.R. said: "Your conservatism is a good thing for us in this Administration." He excelled at evasion. Under the spell of his hearty personality and effervescent smile, people simply forgot what they had come to see him for.

For all his apparent gaiety, however, Roosevelt remained deeply, almost fatalistically religious. He was a vestryman and later Senior Warden of Saint James' Episcopal Church in Hyde Park, but while he was in Washington, he refused to participate in public prayer. "I can do almost everything in the 'Goldfish Bowl' of the President's life," he said, "but I'll be hanged if I can say my prayers in it." Only once did he break his own rule. On D-Day, June 6, 1944, when the massive Allied invasion of Normandy began, Roosevelt went on the radio to read a prayer he had composed for the occasion.

As the Congressional election year of 1934 approached, Roosevelt's enemies charged him with all manner of sins. Waxing theological, Al Smith, for example, accused the President of having "stolen the livery of the church to do the work of the devil." But the Roosevelt Administration, unimpressed, carried on with its work, and New Deal programs continued to shuttle through Congress.

The National Labor Board was established in August, 1933, to support labor's right to bargain collectively and to mediate labor disputes that might arise under the NIRA.

TEXT CONTINUED ON PAGE 82

Henry Morgenthau, Jr., was Secretary of the Treasury, 1934–1945.

The talent Harry Hopkins, left, had for quickly grasping the essentials of a complex situation made him a valued New Deal administrator and Roosevelt's confidant.

Harold L. Ickes was the capable and tempestuous Secretary of the Interior during the Roosevelt era.

MEN AROUND THE PRESIDENT

When Roosevelt moved into the White House in 1933, he assembled a group of advisors united by little more than their devotion to him. Nothing could have been more diverse than the temperaments of the members of his Cabinet or of that ever-changing and ever-influential band of unofficial advisors known as the Brain Trust. Roosevelt so charmed them all—from Morgenthau, his humorless, conservative neighbor on the Hudson, to Hopkins, the irreverent, high-spending Iowan— that each man felt he had convinced the President. Then F.D.R. reached a decision that drew on the best that everyone had told him. For Roosevelt was ever the politician, less interested in a theory than in its application.

Louis Howe (right), a newsman, helped make F.D.R. President.

Among Roosevelt's influential counselors were Rexford Tugwell, above left, and Adolph A. Berle, Jr., center, both economists from the Columbia University faculty. James Farley, right, was an extraordinary politician who organized F.D.R.'s first two presidential campaigns.

TEXT CONTINUED FROM PAGE 79

Prohibition, a clear violation of the citizen's right to drink and a major cause of organized crime and political corruption, was repealed by the states in December.

The Gold Reserve Act of 1934 authorized the President to revalue the dollar at 50 to 60 per cent of its gold content. The act stabilized the value of the dollar, freed the United States from domination by foreign currency, and increased the Treasury's control of credit and money.

In June, 1934, Congress passed the Securities Exchange Act, which authorized the creation of the Securities and Exchange Commission. Henceforth all stock exchanges had to be licensed, and all stocks registered with the commission. The Federal Reserve Board was empowered to limit the extension of credit for speculation. Both these measures were designed to protect stockholders and prevent another stock market crash.

To check abuses in interstate communications by wire, telephone, cable, or radio, a Federal Communications Commission also was created in June. In the same month, Congress passed the National Housing Act, which enabled the government to insure loans made by private firms for home construction and repair.

The year 1935, however, was perhaps the most momentous of the New Deal. In January, after the national elections had resulted in a more progressive Congress, F.D.R. declared that relief was "a narcotic, a subtle destroyer of the human spirit." He said that he was "not willing that the vitality of our people be further sapped by the giving of cash, of market baskets, of a few hours of weekly work cutting grass, raking leaves or picking up papers in the public parks. The Federal Government must and shall quit this business of relief."

Calvin Coolidge or Herbert Hoover might have said the same thing with equal fervor, but they would not have proposed Roosevelt's alternative: a massive public works program, which would employ three and a half million and cost approximately five billion dollars. Roosevelt asked that workers be paid more than they got on relief but less than the going wage, so as not to "encourage the rejection of opportunities for private employment."

In April, 1935, Congress passed a five-billion-dollar Emergency Relief Appropriation, described as "the greatest single appropriation in the history of the United States or any other nation." This law, historian William Leuchtenburg adds, "which permitted Roosevelt to spend this huge sum largely as he saw fit, marked a significant shift of power from Congress to the President." Under the law, the Works Progress Administration, which later was named the Works Projects Administration and became widely known as the WPA, supervised the building of hospitals, schools, and airports. Unemployed actors and writers found work in the Federal Theatre

Project and the Federal Writers' Project; some later became famous.

Under this law, too, the National Youth Administration, over seven years, provided part-time jobs for more than 600,000 college students and one and a half million high school pupils and vocational training and construction jobs for 2,600,000 youths not in school. The WPA employed only three million of the ten million Americans out of work in 1935. But in concept and achievement it was an impressive demonstration of what organized social effort could do to relieve economic crisis. Perhaps more important, it set a lasting precedent for massive Presidential authority.

Another historic measure, the National Labor Relations Act—also known as the Wagner Act—was signed by the President on July 5, 1935. This law for the first time put the full weight of the federal government behind organized labor. Under the act the National Labor Relations Board—previously struck down by a Supreme Court ruling—was reconstituted, and labor's right to bargain with management through elected agents was upheld. Moreover, employers were forbidden to indulge in unfair labor practices, including firing workers because they joined labor unions.

The Public Utilities Holding Company Act, also passed in 1935, struck at the maneuver by big utility companies to fix rates through collusion. The Wealth Tax Act discouraged great concentrations of wealth by in-

creasing surtaxes on incomes of $50,000 per year and over, as well as on inheritances, gifts, and capital profits. The Motor Carrier Act set up standards of safety and regulated the rates charged by bus and truck lines engaged in interstate commerce.

Perhaps the most far-reaching reform of the Roosevelt Administration was the Social Security Act of 1935. This law enabled the President to establish what he had fought for in vain in Albany—a national system of old-age insurance for workers retiring at sixty-five. The insurance was to be financed through taxes levied on wage earners and employers alike. The law also provided for aid to the elderly and needy, to the blind, to dependent mothers, and to neglected children.

A federal-state unemployment insurance system was established, and public health agencies were organized. In Arthur Schlesinger, Jr.'s, words, the Social Security Act, despite administrative flaws and financial inequities, heralded "a new phase of national history," and was "a tremendous break with the inhibitions of the past. The federal government," Schlesinger adds, "was at last charged with the obligation to provide its citizens a measure of protection from the hazards and vicissitudes of life."

The Wagner Act, the Wealth Tax Act, and Social Security aroused even deeper hostility in the big business community. Roosevelt's critics frequently cite the legislation of 1935 as evidence of a major shift to the left by his administration. Moley, a former Roosevelt brain-truster turned conservative, argues that the shift was largely political. Roosevelt and his party chiefs, Moley writes, knew that except for Democratic strength in the cities and the solid South, the party was weak nationally. Roosevelt's key party chief, Edward Flynn, once told Moley:

To remain in power, we must attract some millions, perhaps seven, who are hostile or indifferent to both parties. They believe the Republican Party to be controlled by big business and the Democratic Party by the conservative South. These millions are mostly in the cities. They include racial and religious minorities and labor people. We must attract them by radical programs of social and economic reform.

Moley charges that Roosevelt manipulated the distribution of welfare funds to buy Democratic votes in the cities and courted the Negro vote through mere "gestures against discrimination." Such political chicanery, in addition to Roosevelt's open embrace of the newly organized CIO, led to what Moley calls a "transformation of the Democratic Party" as the enemy of business.

Moley's thesis is not without validity. Roosevelt was, in fact, very vigorously trying to widen the electoral base of his party, as he had been off and on since his defeat as a Vice-Presidential candidate in 1920. There is also some truth in the argument, advanced by others, that Roosevelt was trying to upstage such radicals as Louisiana's rabble-rousing Huey Long, who had won considerable national attention with his "Share the Wealth Clubs" and who had clear national ambitions of his own. Long had compared the blue eagle of Roosevelt's National Recovery Administration to the Nazi swastika and had referred to the New Deal as a fancy name for the same old Hooverism.

Both arguments, however, miss the mark. Roosevelt was no radical. Indeed, he had angered the progressives in Congress by his initial opposition to the Wagner Act and his insistence that employees bear part of the cost of Social Security. A more convincing reason for Roosevelt's increasingly liberal position was his very human reaction to the mounting attacks on his Americanism and criticisms of his "unconstitutional" programs by the business community that he believed he had saved.

As historian Richard Hofstadter points out, F.D.R. felt no less betrayed by his class than they by him.

Some of these people [F.D.R. said] really forget how sick they were. But I know how sick they were. I have their fever charts. I know how the knees of all of our rugged individualists were trembling four years ago and how their hearts fluttered. They came to Washington in great numbers. Washington did not look like a dangerous bureaucracy to them then. Oh, no! It looked like an emergency hospital.

The Roosevelts are reunited after Eleanor's return from a 1934 trip to the Caribbean.

Under the Works Progress Administration American artists decorated many of the federal buildings in Washington. George Biddle, who suggested the program to President Roosevelt—a friend since college —here works on a mural in the Justice Department headquarters.

. . . Some of them are even well enough to throw their crutches at the doctor.

Roosevelt was angered, too, by criticism from the Republican-controlled press. Even the powerful chain of papers owned by William Randolph Hearst, a Democrat, assailed his program as the "Raw Deal," a sinister scheme to "Soak the Successful."

Still more decisive in Roosevelt's stronger progressive stand was the opposition of a staunchly conservative Supreme Court. On May 27, 1935, in the famous "sick chicken" case, the Supreme Court had struck at the heart of the New Deal by declaring the NRA codes unconstitutional. The case concerned two Brooklyn poultry dealers who had been convicted of selling diseased chickens and of violating the Live Poultry Code's wage and hour guidelines. The Court ruled that Congress had delegated excessive power to the NRA and that, in any case, Congress had no constitutional right to regulate *intra*state commerce.

Roosevelt rebuked the Court for its "horse-and-buggy definition of interstate commerce." It was absurd, the President said, to suppose that great national problems could be solved by the forty-eight states individually. These states, acting alone, already had proven unable or unwilling to correct economic injustices and cope with the Depression.

To carry out any twentieth-century program [he said in one fireside chat], we must give the Executive Branch of the Government twentieth-century machinery to work with. I recognize that democratic processes are necessarily and rightly slower than dictatorial processes. But I refuse to believe that democratic processes need be dangerously slow.

In his State of the Union message of January 3, 1936, Roosevelt returned to the attack on big business and the Supreme Court, which had chosen to be its spokesman. "In these latter years," F.D.R. told Congress, "we have witnessed the domination of government by financial and industrial groups, numerically small, but politically dominant. . . ." These groups, Roosevelt declared, had been forced by New Deal reforms to relinquish their power. Government had been returned to the people, and as a result, Roosevelt explained, "we have earned the hatred of entrenched greed." Turning to the high Court, Roosevelt charged that businessmen had stolen "the livery of great national constitutional ideals to serve discredited special interests. . . . [and]

wrongfully seek to carry the property and interests entrusted to them into the arena of partisan politics." He accused this business minority of exploiting for its own purposes "legitimate and highly honored business associations" and engaging in "vast propaganda to spread fear and discord among the people. . . ." He warned that this selfish minority again would try to impose on the whole nation the principles that dominated their businesses and the administrations that they had controlled: "autocracy toward labor, toward stockholders, toward consumer, toward public sentiment."

Roosevelt had hoped vainly to preserve the alliance of businessmen, workers, and farmers, who in their desperation had sought his leadership. Perhaps more than any of his predecessors, he was acutely aware that the President—and the Vice-President— were the only government officials elected by all the people. As such, they must represent no one class over another. The Presidency, as F.D.R. saw it, imposed on him "the duty of analyzing and setting forth national needs and ideals which transcend and cut across all lines of party affiliation."

The frenzied attacks of right-wing Republicans and Democrats alike ended this illusion. Even Socialist Party leader Norman Thomas belittled TVA as state capitalism, called the CCC forced labor—as any good reactionary might—and derided Social Security, with all its faults, as a weak imitation of a real program. If Roosevelt united the country in no other way, he united its radical elements in irrational opposition to the only solution that most Americans would accept: the country's traditional middle way, progress between the extremes of left and right.

In January, 1936, despite ringing minority dissents, the Supreme Court enraged the President and Congress by declaring the Agricultural Adjustment Act unconstitutional. The Court argued that Congress had exceeded its legislative authority; that it had presumed to act as "a parliament of the whole people, subject to no restrictions save such as are self-imposed." The implications of this shocking decision were plain. The Court's wisdom, seasoned with conservatism and old age, was more to be trusted than the majority vote of the people's elected representatives. Moreover, by this and other decisions, the Court backed itself into a corner. It decreed

that neither the federal nor the state government had the right to regulate intrastate commerce. Roosevelt seized on this contradiction during the election of 1936. The "nine old men" of the Court, he declared, were creating a legislative "no-man's-land."

At the Democratic Convention in Philadelphia, Roosevelt was renominated by acclamation. At this convention, too, he almost had a disastrous accident. As he approached the stage to speak, leaning on his son Jimmy's arm, people crowded up to see him.

Under the pressure [writes Arthur Schlesinger, Jr.] the steel brace holding Roosevelt's right leg snapped out of position. To the horror of those near him, the President suddenly toppled over. Mike Reilly of the Secret Service dived and caught

The two top officials of the Justice Department flank eight of the "nine old men" of the Supreme Court. From left to right: Attorney General Mitchell, justices Cardozo, Stone, Sutherland, Van Devanter, Hughes, Brandeis, Butler, Roberts, and Solicitor General Thatcher.

him, his shoulder under Roosevelt's right arm, just before he hit the ground. Meanwhile, the pages of the speech floated from the President's hand into the crowd.

Roosevelt recalled that "it was the most frightful five minutes of my life." The President was brushed clean, and he rearranged the pages of his speech. Then at least visibly tranquil, he addressed the cheering convention.

Americans had conquered their fear of fear, Roosevelt told the convention. But now a new, perhaps greater challenge faced them: the attempt of what he called "economic royalists" to regain control in Washington. The people must stand their ground, for political equality, the mere right to vote, was "meaningless in the face of economic inequality." The "economic royalists," the President declared, "complain that we seek to overthrow the institutions of America. What they really complain of is that we seek to take away their power."

"Governments," Roosevelt admitted, "can err. Presidents do make mistakes but. . . . better the occasional faults of a Government that lives in a spirit of charity than the consistent omissions of a Government frozen in the ice of its own indifference." Then he said in words that subsequently have become famous: "There is a mysterious cycle in human events. To some generations much is given. Of other generations much is expected. This generation of Americans has a rendezvous with destiny."

Running again with Garner, Roosevelt was opposed by the amiable but inept Alf Landon, Republican Governor of Kansas. Landon conducted a high-level campaign of agreeable generalities, but his key aides did not. To Landon's consternation, Herbert Hoover continued to insist that Roosevelt had corrupted capitalism with outright socialism. Another Landon aide charged F.D.R. with "leading us toward Moscow" and alleged that the Democratic Party had been "seized by alien and un-American elements." Landon himself wisely refrained from direct criticism of popular New Deal reforms. He is remembered not only as a gentleman who could lose graciously, but also as the author of one of America's most reassuring campaign statements: "Wherever I have gone in this country," Landon declared, "I have found Americans."

In the greatest victory in the history of American Presidential politics, Roosevelt took every state in the Union except Maine and Vermont. In the popular vote he won by an unprecedented margin—27,752,869 to Landon's 16,674,665. The Electoral College chose him by 523 to 8—the greatest plurality since 1820. The Democratic majority in the Senate—there were 76 Democrats and only 16 Republicans—was the most overwhelming since 1869. Their majority in the House—331 to 89—was the largest since 1855. "As Maine goes," the Democrats cried, "so goes Vermont!" "On the bridge over the

Salmon Falls River, where automobiles crossed from New Hampshire into Maine," writes Arthur Schlesinger, Jr., "someone hung a sign: 'YOU ARE NOW LEAVING THE UNITED STATES.'"

Franklin D. Roosevelt was sworn in for his second term as President on January 20, 1937, under the terms of the newly ratified Twentieth Amendment. It was the 150th anniversary year of the Constitutional Convention. And Roosevelt, in his inaugural address, looked back on his first four years in the White House with pride.

In the 1936 campaign a model of Roosevelt's head corked a bottle celebrating the TVA, while the Republican candidate, Alf Landon, of Kansas, adorned a pin surrounded by a sunflower, emblem of his state.

YEARS OF DUST

RESETTLEMENT ADMINISTRATION
Rescues Victims
Restores Land to Proper Use

"Our progress out of the Depression," he declared, "is obvious." America, he said, had at last set out "upon the road of enduring progress."

But Roosevelt warned that the nation had by no means recovered fully:

I see millions of families trying to live on incomes so meager that the pall of family disaster hangs over them day by day.

I see millions whose daily lives in city and on farm continue under conditions labeled indecent by a so-called polite society half a century ago.

I see millions denied education, recreation, and the opportunity to better their lot and the lot of their children.

I see millions lacking the means to buy the products of farm and factory and by their poverty denying work and productiveness to many other millions.

I see one third of a nation ill-housed, ill-clad, ill-nourished.

Such conditions of want, Roosevelt said, could not be tolerated. And the voters, in their overwhelming endorsement of the New Deal, had indicated clearly that they wanted more effective measures taken to combat those conditions. As for himself, Roosevelt declared: "I assume the solemn obligation of leading the American people forward along the road over which they have chosen to advance."

Armed with the massive vote of confidence, Roosevelt struck out anew

at the greatest foes of the New Deal: the "nine old men" of the Supreme Court—average age, 71. How dare the Court strike down laws passed overwhelmingly by the Congress? The question was, in the President's words, "whether the kind of government which the people of the United States had voted for in 1932, 1934, and 1936 was to be permitted by the Supreme Court to function." Could the "physical conditions of 1787 in farming, labor, manufacturing, mining, industry, and finance" really be expected to be the "yardsticks of legal power" some one hundred fifty years later?

BOTH: MUSEUM OF MODERN ART

Under Roosevelt the government set up agencies to deal with the nation's ills and employed leading artists to publicize the agencies. Ben Shahn created the poster opposite; Lester Beall, the one at right.

93

Roosevelt committed a serious political blunder when he proposed to pack the Supreme Court with his own men. As this 1937 cartoon shows, he was opposed by the public and by the Senate.

The Supreme Court itself was guilty of unconstitutional action in usurping the power of Congress and acting like a "super-legislature." More than that, Roosevelt said, it was forcing the Constitution into a straitjacket; the Constitution that purposely had been made flexible—"so simple and practical that it is possible to meet extraordinary needs . . . without loss of essential form." The Constitution had functioned in crisis under thirty-one presidents. Why was the Court determined to cripple it under him?

Without consulting even Democratic leaders in Congress, Roosevelt proposed a law that would give the President the right to appoint one new justice—up to a limit of six—for each justice who failed to retire six months after reaching the age of seventy. The proposed law would have effectively eliminated any judicial check on administration policies or laws passed by the New Deal Congress.

Roosevelt was at the peak of his popularity, but the court-packing plan was a blunder that cost him considerable support. Not only was it a shocking violation of the federal principle of the separation of executive, judicial, and legislative powers—the central pillar of American democracy—but also it gave ammunition to those critics who had pictured Roosevelt as a destroyer of the Constitution. Not even the solid Democratic majority in the Congress was united in support of the President's original plan, which was voted down 10–8 by

the Senate Judiciary Committee before it even reached the floor. Liberal and conservative critics were equally outraged by the plan. A segregationist President, one liberal declared, "could pack the Supreme Court so that no Negro could get within a thousand miles of justice," while Carter Glass, the Senator from Virginia, thought that it would favor integration.

One effect of the furor, however, was modification of the Court's stand on New Deal measures. Doubtless well aware of the mounting public anger over its obstructionism, the Court upheld Social Security, if only by a margin of 5–4. By 1940, resignations and new appointments by Roosevelt had created a Court largely sympathetic to the New Deal.

Historian Richard Hofstadter has noted "Roosevelt's confidence that even when he was operating in unfamiliar territory he could do no wrong, commit no serious mistakes." This confidence had taken him successfully through his first turbulent term of experiment and reform—this confidence and an inborn optimism so great, one Cabinet member said, that "nothing could touch him." However, in his attempt to unseat the Supreme Court, Roosevelt had drastically altered his Presidential image. He no longer seemed above the political fray, immune to its pettiness and its backroom deals.

Republican progressive William Allen White, a highly respected Midwest journalist, spoke for most people who felt that Roosevelt had over-played his hand: "Assuming," White said, "which is not at all impossible, a reactionary president, as charming, as eloquent and as irresistible as Roosevelt, with power to change the court, and we should be in the devil's own fix if he decided to abridge the bill of rights by legislation which he could easily call emergency legislation."

F.D.R. lost further prestige by personally intervening in the Congressional elections of 1938. He took to the campaign trail, determined to punish senators and congressmen who had opposed him on the Court plan and on other New Deal measures. But he failed to unseat hostile congressmen or senators, except in one contest. More than that, seventy-five new Republicans were elected to the House and seven to the Senate.

By the end of 1938, Roosevelt still might thunder about "the power of the few to manage the economic life of the nation," but the fact remains that the New Deal was running out of steam. In 1938, to be sure, the Second Agricultural Adjustment Act was passed, guaranteeing fixed commodity prices and extending loans to farmers who limited crop planting. The Fair Labor Standards Act established guidelines for minimum wages and maximum hours and banned child labor in the manufacture of goods shipped from one state to another. A recession in the same year was checked at least partially by massive government spending. But after five years

of Roosevelt's New Deal, 7,500,000 Americans still were unemployed.

In his first term and in part of his second as President, Roosevelt was preoccupied with domestic affairs. Even in foreign policy, however, he had moved cautiously away from the pious isolationism that had characterized American conduct in the world since the Harding era and the United States' refusal to enter the League of Nations. On November 16, 1933, the United States faced up to reality and extended diplomatic recognition to the sixteen-year-old government of the Soviet Union.

Ironically, Roosevelt's strongest supporters were American industrialists and bankers who knew a good market when they saw one. Reactionaries predicted that a wave of Bolshevism would inundate the United States, which prompted one newspaper tycoon to say, "I think the menace of Bolshevism in the United States is about as great as the menace of sunstroke in Greenland or chilblains in the Sahara."

In May, 1934, the United States gave up its treaty right to intervene in Cuba in time of disorder. It was a clause despised by the Cubans, for in effect it meant that the United States could virtually dictate Cuban internal policies. Roosevelt announced a "Good Neighbor" policy toward all of Latin America, renounced the option of armed intervention for which America was despised throughout the continent, removed U.S. Marines

In South America in 1936, Roosevelt bids farewell to Uruguay's President Gabriel Terra.

from Haiti, promised not to intervene in Panamanian affairs, and negotiated mutually beneficial trade agreements with Latin American countries. When F.D.R. visited Latin America in 1936, he received a rousing welcome as "el gran democrata," architect of TVA and the kind of social reforms that Latins wanted for themselves.

In general, however, for approximately six years after Roosevelt took office, Americans were too busy pulling themselves out of the Depression to give much attention to world affairs. They were only dimly aware that an economically depressed Europe had turned increasingly to dictatorship. In Germany, Adolf Hitler was rising to power. In Italy, Benito Mus-solini ruled a Fascist state. In Japan, the militarists were in command. These three nations were to form an alliance, the Axis, which in a few, shocking years would plunge mankind into the living hell of World War II.

In meeting this fanatic challenge to liberty and civilization, America again would look to "that man in the White House," the man who had conquered first his own fear, then theirs. Roosevelt already had won a great place in history by battling the Depression. He would assure it by leading his nation to victory in its most awesome war. For the former mama's boy of Groton and Harvard, for the country gentleman of Hyde Park, a still greater challenge was at hand.

THE UBIQUITOUS MRS. ROOSEVELT

Rexford Tugwell recalls that for Eleanor Roosevelt "a person was simply a person . . . . All were equally entitled to life, to justice, and to happiness." Eleanor devoted herself to seeing that those rights became realities. Shy, humorless, and totally sincere, she gave up her private life without complaint when Franklin became President and put her inexhaustible good health and energy to work doing good. She became a familiar and sympathetic figure to millions through her many lectures, her daily syndicated newspaper column, "My Day," and her constant travels around the United States during the Depression and all over the world during and after the war.

© The New Yorker

One amazed miner tells the other: "For gosh sakes, here comes Mrs. Roosevelt."

At Hyde Park, opposite, Eleanor and the President share a rare moment of solitude.

TIME–LIFE INC.; PHOTO, THOMAS MC AVOY

The First Lady greets actress Lucille Ball.

WIDE WORLD

Mrs. R. helps in a Depression soup kitchen.

If Eleanor's life could be summed up in a word, it surely would be "participation." She appeared to be equally at ease rubbing noses with a New Zealand Maori in a traditional gesture of welcome and attending a party at the White House for the President's military guard.

Reluctantly but successfully, Eleanor traveled to the Democratic Convention in Chicago in 1940 to assure the nomination of Henry Wallace, her husband's choice as his running mate.

5

DEMOCRACY'S CHAMPION

Adolf Hitler never made a secret of his plans for world conquest. His blueprint, *Mein Kampf,* was published in 1925 and an English translation was available as early as 1933. But few people, even among the loyal Nazis who were ordered to buy it, actually read the book. Those who did, throughout the world, found it difficult to take seriously "that silly book" by a former Austrian paper hanger. The only believers were that hard core of Nazi henchmen who shared Hitler's vision of world empire.

In his astonishing testament, Adolf Hitler's deranged mind and dictatorial plans were exposed for all who cared to see: his concept of the "Aryan" superman destined by superior intelligence and physical splendor to rule racial inferiors; his denunciation of religion as effeminate and democracy as decadent; his glorification of the

The collaboration of Roosevelt and Winston Churchill, England's Prime Minister, helped the free world through a dark time.

warrior as the noblest expression of the human spirit; his insane portrait of a Jewish world conspiracy. In a speech published in 1934, Hitler said that the objective of his Nazi movement was no less than "international world-wide despotism . . . or the Holy Reich of the German nation!" He dreamed of "the rule of the superior race over the whole world for at least 1,000 to 2,000 years."

With the triumph of the Nazi Party in Germany in the spring and summer of 1933, during Roosevelt's first term as President, the deadly seriousness of Hitler's blueprint for world conquest had been made clear. It was equally clear to students of the Far East that Japan, not content with the conquest of China, envisioned a vast Pacific empire, embracing not only Dutch, French, and English colonial possessions, but America's Philippine Islands as well. As Assistant Secretary of the Navy, Roosevelt had been alarmed by the growing arms race between Tokyo and Wash-

Roosevelt got on very well with George VI when the King and Queen of England paid an official visit to America during Western Europe's last summer of peace before World War II.

ington and had predicted that there would ultimately be a conflict between the United States and Japan.

Preoccupied with their own domestic problems, most Americans in the thirties paid little heed to the dictatorships that had engulfed Europe. The America First Committee, an isolationist group that included some leading citizens, insisted that America should not intervene in the "sordid" affairs of a corrupt Europe; that America, protected by vast oceans from the Nazi and Japanese dictators, could go it alone. An openly pro-Hitler organization, the German-American Bund, saluted the Führer who had assured them in *Mein Kampf* that they would remain masters of "the American continent . . . as long as [the German-American] does not fall victim to defilement of the blood."

In this climate of fanaticism, isolationism, and tragic nonsense, in this nation that never had lost a war and was convinced of its invulnerability, President Roosevelt's warning voice fell on deaf ears. Americans, he said, "imagine that if the civilization of Europe is about to destroy itself through internal strife, it might just as well go ahead and do it and that the

When the British royal couple arrived, the temperature in the capital was 94°. Elizabeth, the Queen, was luckier than her husband, for at least she could raise a parasol against the sun.

United States can stand idly by."

For a long time Britain and France seemed oblivious to the Nazi threat. Hitler's occupation of the Rhineland in March, 1936, his alliance with Italy's Benito Mussolini in the fall of that year, his formation of the Berlin-Rome-Tokyo "Axis" soon afterward, and his brazen annexation of Austria in March, 1938, failed to stir London and Paris to action. In September, 1938, Prime Minister Neville Chamberlain, fresh from his celebrated appeasement of the Führer in Munich, announced to cheering Englishmen that the agreement he had just finished signing with Hitler meant no less than "peace for our time."

Roosevelt did not share Chamberlain's optimism.

Let no one imagine [he warned a Chicago audience a year before Munich] that America will escape [the Axis terror], that this western hemisphere . . . will continue tranquilly and peacefully to carry on the ethics and arts of civilization. . . . The peace-loving nations must make a concerted effort in opposition to those violations of treaties and those ignorings of human instincts which today are creating a state of international anarchy and instability from which there is no escape through mere isolation or neutrality.

In this historic address, Roosevelt compared the rise of the Axis powers to an epidemic. At such a time, the President said, the wise community "joins in a quarantine of the patients in order to protect the health of the community against the spread of the disease." While Roosevelt appeased American neutralists by adding that "we are determined to keep out of war," he warned that "we cannot insure ourselves against the disastrous effects of war and the dangers of involvement. . . . We cannot have complete protection in a world of disorder in which confidence and security have broken down. . . ." To Colonel Edward House, Woodrow Wilson's friend and advisor, the President wrote: "War will be a greater danger to us if we

close all the doors and windows than if we go out in the street and use our influence to curb the riot."

Unmistakably, Roosevelt was advocating a collective break in diplomatic relations with the Axis. Under pressure from the isolationists and neutralists, however, F.D.R. backed down, denying that he had advocated any change in America's official policy of neutrality in the world conflict. When the Munich pact was signed a year later, in effect giving Czechoslovakia to Hitler, he wrote Canada's Prime Minister MacKenzie King: "We in the United States rejoice with

In 1934, while Roosevelt coped with the Depression in America, Adolf Hitler consolidated his power over Germany at Nazi party gatherings like this one at Nürnberg.

you, and the world at large, that the outbreak of war was averted."

Roosevelt soon reverted to his basically pessimistic view of the Axis, however, when he warned of the danger of "peace by fear," the folly of a policy of appeasement, which merely had increased Hitler's appetite for power with every new concession to his greed. In his State of the Union message in January, 1939, he was more specific: "There comes a time in the affairs of men," he told Congress, "when they must prepare to defend not their homes alone but the tenets of faith and humanity on which their churches, their governments, and their very civilization are founded." To Americans, he said, "much is given; more is expected. This generation will nobly save or meanly lose the last best hope of earth."

In April, 1939, Roosevelt signed a bill allocating $549 million for national defense, including the strengthening of United States bases in the Pacific and the Caribbean. That same month he made a personal appeal to Hitler and Mussolini to abandon their plans for world conquest. Hitler replied in August by signing a nonaggression pact with the Soviet Union that shocked the world and on September 1 by invading Poland. Even when Britain and France declared war

A German soldier hurls a potato-masher grenade in Poland, the first country to fall before Hitler's massive "blitzkrieg" attacks.

on Germany and Nazi bombs rained on Warsaw, the United States again solemnly proclaimed its neutrality.

Congress initially refused even Roosevelt's request that the Neutrality Act of 1937 be amended to permit the sale of arms to the Allies. As it stood, the President argued, the policy of neutrality could aid only Hitler. Reluctantly, Congress agreed to sell arms to belligerents on a strict "cash-and-carry" basis. It also forbade Americans to travel on belligerent ships. By May, 1940, Hitler had conquered Belgium, Denmark, Norway, and the Netherlands; in June the British completed the evacuation of Dunkirk and Paris fell to the Nazis.

In July Congress authorized the expenditure of $4 billion to build a two-ocean navy. Two months later, bypassing a reluctant Congress, Roosevelt himself gave fifty over-age destroyers to Britain in exchange for 99-year leases on eight bases from Newfoundland to British Guiana. And by October, sixteen million Americans had registered for military training under the Selective Service Act, the first "peacetime" draft in the history of the United States.

At home Roosevelt faced a major economic recession and frantic conservative opposition to his decision to seek an unprecedented third term as President in 1940. The "Roosevelt Recession" hit the nation on October 19, 1937, when over seven and one quarter million shares were traded on the New York stock market:

the biggest total [writes Frederick Lewis Allen] since the collapse of the New Deal Honeymoon bull market in the summer of 1933. . . . Only the fact that speculation previous to August had been moderate and well-margined, with the SEC watching carefully to prevent manipulation, kept the annihilation of values from having disastrous consequences outside the exchanges. . . . Not until the end of March, 1938, did the stock market touch bottom. . . .

The recession was caused by inflationary pressures on prices and wages, a drop in new investments and purchasing power, therefore in production, and an almost complete end of massive government spending. Two million lost their jobs within a few months. Ironically, Roosevelt reacted initially much as Herbert Hoover had. "Everything will work out all right," he assured his Cabinet, "if we just sit tight and keep quiet." In addressing a special session of Congress in November, 1937, Roosevelt conceded "a marked recession," but he denied that it was one of serious proportions.

The following April, however, Roosevelt asked Congress to authorize a three-billion-dollar program of federal relief, including public works and housing. Enriched by this government pump-priming, the economy rallied. But only war and huge government defense contracts for industry would bring America even close to full employment.

There was strong public sentiment that Roosevelt should accept the Democratic nomination for the third time because of the firm leadership that he would provide in the coming confrontation with the Axis powers. There was also, however, strong sentiment against his breaking a tradition dating back to George Washington, who had declined a third term. Vice-President Garner and Democratic National Committee Chairman James Farley not only objected to the third term in principle, but also were actively seeking the Presidency for themselves.

At first, Roosevelt maintained a calculated silence, hinting only that he would accept a genuine party draft to serve again. But by early July, he had made up his mind. "Jim," he told an angry Farley, "if nominated and elected, I could not in these times refuse to take the inaugural oath, even if I knew I would be dead within thirty days."

Outraged conservatives called F.D.R. a new Caesar, another Hitler. Even genial Alf Landon declared: "The tradition against the perpetuation in office of the Chief Executive is as sacred as anything the American boy learns at his mother's knee. . . . The third term is fatal to the future of the republic . . . and not American." Others argued, however, that the Constitution said nothing about Presidential terms and that Washington himself had said that he saw no reason why a President should not serve in an emergency as long as his leadership was needed or desired. Secretary of the Interior Harold L. Ickes put it more plainly: "If the peo-

Roosevelt's decision to seek a third term as President in 1940, thus breaking with a tradition set by George Washington, aroused a storm of conflicting feelings in the United States. As this cartoon indicates, some felt that he was seeking to become a dictator like Hitler.

ple," protected by a free press, the Congress, and the courts, "want President Roosevelt for another four years, they are well within their rights in taking him."

There is much evidence that Roosevelt sought a third term in large measure because he felt that by stepping down he would be helping the Axis powers. In late June, 1940, Japan had invaded French Indochina. In July Hitler's air force began its merciless bombing of Britain and arrogantly proclaimed an imminent invasion across the English Channel. Roosevelt also was aware that Germany was trying to create an atomic bomb, and he had given American scientists the go-ahead on a similar project. He felt that he could not lightly relinquish his firm commitments to the national defense. Nor did he believe that either Farley or Garner was qualified to be President. After an unimpressive challenge by Farley and Garner, Roosevelt was nominated for a third term by the Democratic Convention in Chicago on July 17, 1940. Henry A. Wallace of Iowa, an articulate liberal with broad appeal to the farm belt, was chosen as his running mate.

Some people derided Wendell Willkie, the Republican candidate, as a dude or "the barefoot boy of Wall Street." But historian John Gunther has called him "one of the most lovable, most gallant, most zealous, and most forward-looking Americans of this—or any—time." He had secured the Republican nomination on the sixth ballot after strong challenges by Thomas E. Dewey and Robert A. Taft. Willkie was a moderate businessman, bitterly opposed by Republican bosses for his admission that America could not safely stay aloof from world conflict and for his open support of major New Deal programs. Indeed, Willkie had been a delegate to the Democratic Convention of 1924, had voted for Roosevelt in 1932, and considered himself a Democrat until 1938. The Democrats realized that a man with such a background might command broad popular support.

It was a mean, often vicious campaign. Reactionaries assailed Roosevelt in turn for warmongering and for not arming America rapidly enough. Even Willkie, bowing to right-wing Republican pressure, condemned Roosevelt's destroyer deal with Britain as "the most dictatorial act ever taken by an American President." In his final campaign broadcast he went so far as to affirm that Roosevelt's re-election would be "the last step in the destruction of our democracy. . . ."

Willkie was ill-served by the extremists and hatemongers who backed him. Charles A. Lindbergh shocked millions by urging co-operation with Hitler if he should win the war in Europe. Right-wing radicals joined the Communists in denouncing Roosevelt's "despotism." Herbert Hoover declared that America's entry into the war under Roosevelt would mean dictatorship in the United States. Al

Smith, ever unforgiving, called his old friend "the chief apostle of class hatred in the United States." And labor chief John L. Lewis of the CIO said that the President was a "traitor to labor."

The Democratic campaign was not much more elevated in tone. At first, Roosevelt maintained a studied image as the Commander in Chief, above politics. "Events move so fast in other parts of the world," he announced both grandly and accurately, "that it has become my duty to remain either in the White House itself or at some nearby point . . .—where, if need be, I can be back at my desk in the space of a very few hours." He added archly that he would "not have the time or the inclination to engage in purely political debate."

In time-honored political tradition, Roosevelt left the name-calling and precinct infighting to his party lieutenants, notably Henry Wallace. The Democratic vice-presidential candidate denounced Willkie as "well-meaning, confused, and supported by Nazi agents." At a Madison Square Garden rally of the American Labor Party, Wallace announced, incredibly, that Hitler himself wanted Willkie to defeat Roosevelt. Nor was the President above such tactics. "To a press conference early in October," writes James MacGregor Burns, a Roosevelt biographer, "the President brought a New York *Times* dispatch from Rome reporting that the Axis hoped for Roosevelt's defeat. He would not

comment. 'I am just quoting the press at you,' . . ." Roosevelt said. A sordid whispering campaign focused on Willkie's German ancestry. As he campaigned, the friendly Republican was pelted with eggs and stones by jeering workers. Republican sloganeers urged Americans to strike F.D.R. out "at third"; but Democrats countered with such nonsense as "Better a Third-Termer than a Third-Rater."

Straining for a winning issue, Willkie, to his discredit, joined the radicals in their attack on Roosevelt as a warmonger. He belied his own beliefs when he said: "If [Roosevelt's] promise to keep our boys out of foreign wars is no better than his promise to balance the budget, they're already on the transports." It was a shattering about-face for Willkie, who had publicly supported Roosevelt's policy of aid to the Allies "short of war."

Willkie's increasingly barbed attacks and his growing strength in opinion polls alarmed F.D.R. In the last two weeks of the campaign the President dropped the mantle of state and took to the hustings. To a roaring Philadelphia crowd he declared: "I am an old campaigner, and I love a good fight." Then, in Boston, he announced: "And while I am talking to you mothers and fathers, I give you one more assurance. I have said this before, but I shall say it again and again and again, your boys are not going to be sent into any foreign wars."

Now F.D.R. tore into the Republican record. He was, in the words of

James MacGregor Burns, "in turn intimate, ironic, bitter, sly, sarcastic, indignant, solemn." He reminded Americans of the darkest days of the Depression and what the New Deal had done for them. "Back in 1932," he declared, Republican leaders had been "willing to let workers starve if they could not get a job." Republican leaders had opposed a minimum wage law, unemployment insurance, even the right of unions to bargain for fair wages and hours. Recalling the Veterans' Bonus March on the Capitol, he reminded an enormous radio audience that the Republican leaders had "met the demands of unemployed veterans with troops and tanks." The Republicans had gone down to defeat with such inhuman and repressive policies, Roosevelt said, and now they were singing a different tune, a tune

Republican candidate Wendell Willkie lost the 1940 election to Roosevelt after a hard-fought campaign. But Willkie clearly was popular in his home town of Elwood, Indiana, left, where he accepted the nomination.

arranged just for votes. As for those Republicans now screaming about America's inadequate military defenses, Roosevelt asked, why had they opposed his defense proposals every step of the way? They had called him a warmonger because he had insisted on arming America to meet an inevitable Nazi challenge. These Republicans, the President declared, had executed "a remarkable somersault. I wonder if the election could have something to do with it."

The closing weeks of the campaign, for all of Roosevelt's bravado, were conducted in a growing atmosphere of apprehension and fear of war. Under the Selective Service Act sixteen million had registered for military training, and on October 29, just one week before the election, Secretary of War Henry L. Stimson drew

115

from the "goldfish bowl" the names of the first men destined for boot camp.

On November 5, 1940, fifty million Americans went to the polls. The campaign had been cruelly divisive at precisely the moment when America had been most in need of unity. The closing opinion polls had shown Willkie cutting his lead, and Roosevelt waited at Hyde Park in apprehension, watching the returns trickle in, unwilling to see even his closest aides.

He had much to think about: the defection of trusted lieutenants like Farley and Garner; the stubborn opposition of the overwhelmingly Republican press; the future of his New

As the nation prepared for war, isolationist mothers knelt on a Washington street to protest the Lend-Lease Act (Bill 1776), and Secretary of War Henry Stimson chose the number of the first peacetime draftee.

Deal programs should the Republicans be elected; the alliance of left- and right-wing extremists joined only by their hatred of him; the future of the American defense program in the hands of men who were willing to let Hitler go his way unchallenged or who openly supported him; the wisdom of his decision even to seek a third term. Had Eleanor been right when she urged him not to run? He was, in fact, tired. He had hinted to Farley that another four years in the White House, particularly if war should come, might prove too much for him physically.

As the final returns poured in, particularly from heavily populated industrial areas where the memory of the Depression was keenest, there was no doubt that Franklin Delano Roosevelt was still the choice of an overwhelming majority of Americans. Roosevelt defeated Willkie in an Electoral College landslide of 449 to 82. He won by a popular margin of almost five million votes, 27,307,819 to 22,321,018.

Willkie made history of his own, however, in a statesmanlike, even noble, radio address conceding defeat. It did much to heal the serious wounds of the campaign. "Although constitutional government had been blotted out elsewhere," Willkie declared, "here in America men and women kept it triumphantly alive. No matter which side you were on, this great expression of faith in the free system of government must have given hope wherever man hopes to be free." Discounting caustic comments made in the heat of campaigning, Willkie added: "There is no bitterness in my heart; I hope there is none in yours. We have elected Franklin D. Roosevelt President. He is your President. He is my President. . . . And we will pray God may guide his hand during the next four years. . . ."

The warmth of Willkie's speech of concession was without parallel in American history. Its eloquent recognition of the need for national unity in the impending world crisis was vastly reassuring to the man who once again was called to lead the United States. Roosevelt later named Willkie his personal ambassador on fact-finding, good-will visits to world capitals. Willkie also aided Roosevelt by enlisting the support of his fellow Republicans for national defense policies that both men considered to be above party politics.

The Indiana Republican must be credited with the first major step toward that bipartisanship on foreign policy that was to become the touchstone of American unity at home and victory abroad.

On January 20, 1941, Franklin D. Roosevelt took the presidential oath of office for the third time. As he administered the oath, stately Chief Justice Charles Evans Hughes quipped: "Mr. President, this is getting to be a habit." While delivering his inaugural address, however, the President was solemnity itself:

In Washington's day [he said] the task of the people was to create and weld together a nation.

In Lincoln's day the task of the people was to preserve that Nation from disruption from within.

In this day the task of the people is to save the Nation and its institutions from disruption from without. . . .

Alluding to the Axis dictators, the President said: "There are men who believe that democracy . . . is limited or measured by a kind of mystical and artificial fate—that, for some unexplained reason, tyranny and slavery have become the surging wave of the future—and that freedom is an ebbing tide."

However, America's victory over the Depression and its conquest of fear through its traditional democratic institutions, Roosevelt said, had proven the enemies of democracy wrong. In the boldest challenge he had yet made to the Axis powers, Roosevelt warned Americans of the "real peril of inaction" and isolation on the world stage. He warned, too, of "great perils never before encountered." He pleaded with Americans to heed the voices of "those across the seas—the enslaved, as well as the free." And more boldly still, in a virtual call to arms, he urged a "muster" of the spirit of America in "the cause of national defense." His concluding words were meant, too, for Hitler, for Mussolini, and for the Japanese warlords: "We do not retreat. We are not content to stand still. As Americans, we go forward, in the service of our country, by the will of God."

Roosevelt had not waited for his third inaugural to alert Americans to the national danger. In a fireside chat on December 29, 1940, he had urged the nation to become an "arsenal of democracy," to give military supplies, food, and support to those abroad already fighting the first round of America's fight for freedom. In his State of the Union message on January 6, 1941, he returned to the point: "Today, thinking of our children and their children, we oppose enforced isolation for ourselves or for any part of the Americas." No nation could remain either safe or free, he said, unless protected by a united world order founded on "four essential freedoms": freedom of speech, freedom of worship, freedom from want, and freedom from fear.

In the same historic address, Roosevelt asked Congress to empower him to sell, lease, transfer, or arrange exchanges of arms, food, and raw materials to nations fighting the Axis powers. The Lend-Lease Act, passed in March, 1941, with Willkie's assistance on Capitol Hill, was, in one historian's words, "a milestone in the organizing of world resistance to Hitler."

The United States now moved with undisguised speed to build up its defenses. In April, by arrangement with Denmark, American bases were built on Greenland. Roosevelt enlarged the United States patrol zone in the North Atlantic to protect convoys to Britain against Nazi submarines. In May he ordered the construction of a gigantic strategic bomber command, and following an increase in Nazi submarine "incidents," proclaimed an "unlimited national emergency." In June German and Italian consulates were ordered to close throughout the United States and Nazi officials were ordered to leave the country.

Soon after Hitler attacked the Soviet Union on June 22, American lend-lease aid was dispatched to the Russians. In July United States troops replaced British forces at naval and air bases in Iceland, as part of America's undeclared war on Nazi subs. In the same month, as Japan marched through French Indochina, systematically extending its empire throughout the Far East, Roosevelt halted trade with the Japanese, froze their assets in America, accepted the Philippine Army into the United States armed forces, and named General Douglas MacArthur as American commander in the Far East.

Between August 9 and 12, 1941, President Roosevelt and Prime Minister Churchill met secretly aboard the American cruiser *Augusta* and the British *Prince of Wales* off Newfoundland. The meeting was called primarily to discuss military strategy and supply. But out of it emerged the historic document known as The Atlantic Charter, announced to the world on August 14. Recognizing "the dangers to world civilization arising from the policies of military domina-

tion by conquest" by the Axis powers, the President and the Prime Minister issued a joint declaration of the principles that would guide them in meeting the Axis challenge. Both nations announced that they sought "no aggrandizement, territorial or other." They opposed "territorial changes that do not accord with the freely expressed wishes of the people concerned." They affirmed the policy of self-determination of nations and pledged to build a system of world trade that would further the economic prosperity of "all States, great and small, victor or vanquished. . . ."

Every effort would be expended "to bring about the fullest collaboration between all nations in the economic field with the object of securing, for all, improved labor standards, economic adjustment and social security." They looked forward to a world at peace in which "all the men in all the lands may live out their lives in freedom from fear and want." They asserted the right of all men to freedom of the seas. Finally, they stated, "all of the nations of the world, for realistic as well as spiritual reasons, must come to the abandonment of the use of force. . . ." "Pending the establishment of a wider and permanent system of general security," they urged

Roosevelt and Churchill sing "Onward, Christian Soldiers" during Sunday services aboard the British battleship Prince of Wales *anchored off Newfoundland. At this meeting in 1941 they drafted the Atlantic Charter.*

disarmament once the Axis powers were crushed, and "all other practicable measures which will lighten for peace-loving peoples the crushing burden of armaments."

The Charter, often cited as the ideological foundation of the United Nations, was a ringing manifesto hailed throughout the free world. More than that, it sealed America's alliance with England and gave friend and foe alike new evidence of America's firmness.

Less than one month after the Charter was issued, the United States destroyer *Greer,* while trailing a Nazi sub in the North Atlantic, was torpedoed, but not sunk, by the Germans. In a fireside chat that later was broadcast around the world, an angry Roosevelt warned that Americans must be deceived no longer by the "tender whisperings of appeasers that Hitler is not interested in the Western Hemisphere," or by "lullabies that a wide ocean protects us from him." Thereafter, the President declared, German and Italian vessels entered American waters at their own peril; the United States would shoot them on sight. By

On December 6, 1941, Roosevelt sent this message to Emperor Hirohito of Japan in a last, futile attempt to avert war. At dawn on the following day the Japanese attacked Pearl Harbor.

I address myself to Your Majesty at this moment in the fervent hope that Your Majesty may, as I am doing, give thought in this definite emergency to ways of dispelling the dark clouds. I am confident that both of us, for the sake of the peoples not only of our own great countries but for the sake of humanity in neighboring territories, have a sacred duty to restore traditional amity and prevent further death and destruction in the world.

Franklin D Roosevelt

****

November, even ships of the American merchant fleet had been armed.

Roosevelt moved with similar speed to negotiate an understanding with Japan that might at least avert war. In late September, 1940, after Japan's occupation of Indochina and its military alliance with Germany and Italy, F.D.R. imposed an embargo on American shipments of iron and scrap steel to Japan. In July, 1941, he froze Japanese assets in the United States and joined an Allied embargo on all oil exports to Japan.

With the fall of Premier Fumimaro Konoye's moderate government in mid-October, 1941, and the rise of the fascistic General Hideki Tojo, the Japanese military junta ruled unchallenged. On November 5 the Tojo government secretly prepared two plans for presentation to Washington to "settle" American-Japanese differences. Each bore a twenty-day deadline and contained demands that Tojo knew the United States would not accept. On the same day Tojo informed the Japanese Navy: "War with the Netherlands, America, England, inevitable; general operational preparations to be completed by early December."

Among Tojo's conditions were an end to the United States embargo, cessation of all American aid to China, and assistance to the Japanese in obtaining the new raw materials it needed to build its empire. American demands, including the surrender of all areas Japan had seized in China and Indochina in exchange for the resumption of trade with America, were equally unacceptable to Tojo. On the day the American offer was made to Japanese diplomats in Washington, a Japanese task force, including two battleships, six aircraft carriers, three cruisers, and nine destroyers, started eastward across the Pacific.

In Washington, meanwhile, the diplomatic minuet continued, with no movement on either side toward genuine negotiation. Both powers clearly were stalling for time. Indeed, convinced that war was imminent, Washington had alerted U.S. Pacific commanders to be ready for combat as early as November 27. There could be no doubt of Japan's intentions, for the United States had broken the Japanese code months before. "I think I can baby the Japs along for another three months," Roosevelt had told Churchill aboard the *Augusta*. The U.S. Joint Chiefs of Staff, anxious to build American defenses, concurred in the President's policy of cordial deception.

Roosevelt's estimate of Japanese strategy was close to the target. On December 2, 1941, after rejecting America's demands, Tokyo sent a coded radio message to the flagship of Vice-Admiral Chuichi Nagumo, sailing one day west of the international dateline.

The message was short: "Climb Mount Niitaka." That message would shatter forever the dream of American neutrality in a world of dictators.

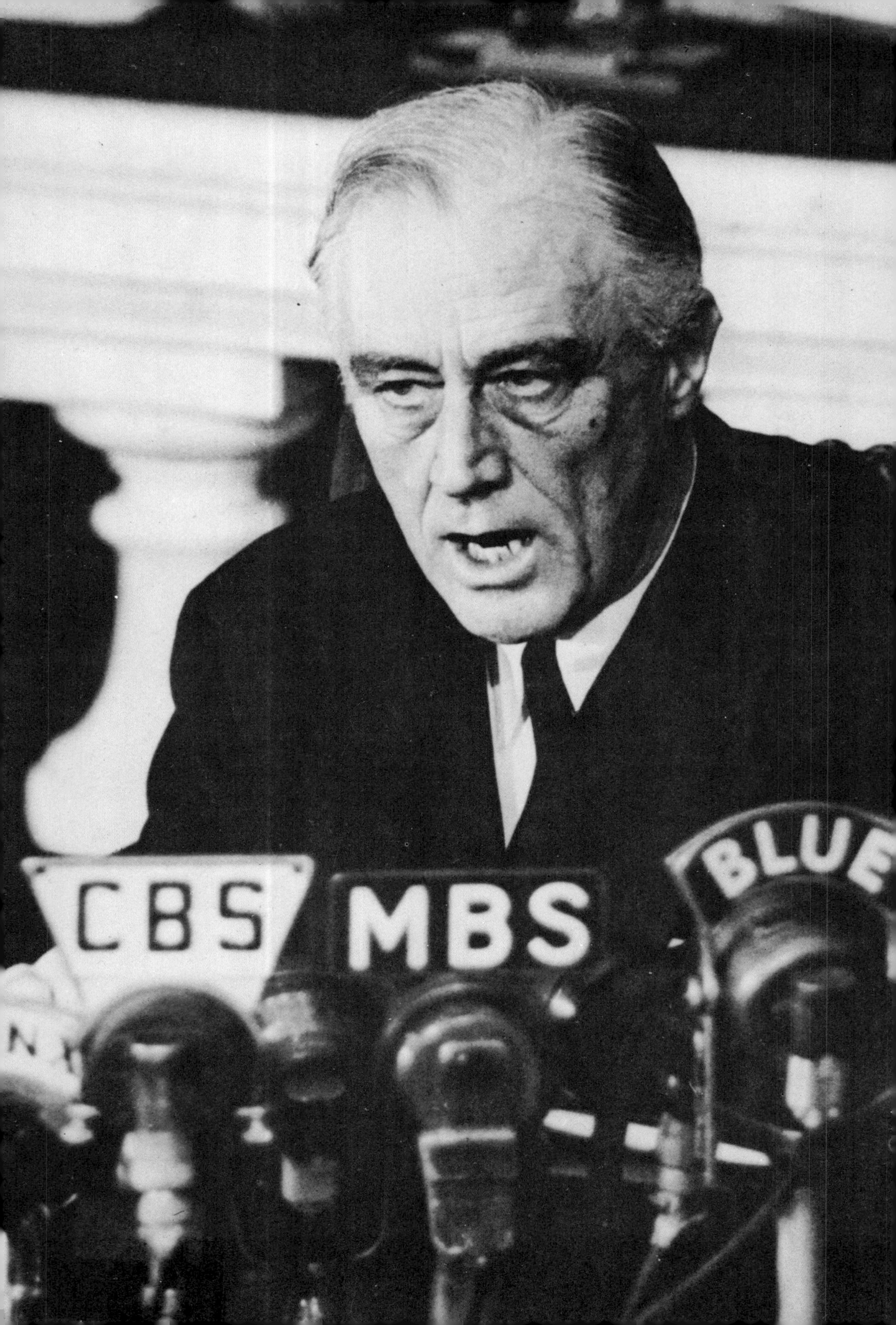
CBS
MBS
BLUE

6

COMMANDER IN CHIEF

Roosevelt's Cabinet had agreed in late November, 1941, to go to war if Japan attacked Malaya or the Dutch East Indies. But even General Douglas MacArthur, with headquarters in the Philippines, did not expect the Japanese to make a move earlier than April of the following year. Even after the final coded message was received from Tojo announcing that Tokyo considered it "impossible to reach an agreement through further negotiations," Roosevelt remained hopeful that his vast powers of persuasion could avert war. On the night of December 6, he sent a personal message to Emperor Hirohito asking him to rebuke the Japanese militarists and keep the peace.

On Sunday, December 7, President Roosevelt had finished lunch and had decided to work on his stamp collec-

Returning from Yalta exhausted, Roosevelt for once remained seated while addressing Congress. Barely six weeks later, he died.

tion when the telephone rang at 1:47 P.M. The White House operator said the caller had insisted on being put through directly to him. It was Secretary of the Navy Frank Knox, informing the President that the Japanese task force sailing under Admiral Nagumo had not "climbed Mount Niitaka" but had attacked the United States Naval Air Base at Pearl Harbor, Hawaii. Launched from carriers 275 miles away, Japanese bombers had found the American fortress, as one Japanese commander put it, "asleep in the morning mist." The sneak attack had taken place at 7:55 A.M., Hawaii time.

When the bombers had flown off, 2,403 Americans were dead and 1,178 were wounded, 300 planes had been destroyed or damaged, six battleships had been sunk or crippled, and several destroyers and cruisers had been destroyed or damaged. Virtually the entire battle line of the American Pacific fleet had been inactivated. Later, General MacArthur's bombers

in the Philippines were destroyed on the ground.

Historian Samuel Eliot Morison has called Pearl Harbor a disaster that "shook the United States as nothing had since the firing on Fort Sumter." Every man, woman, and child who could grasp the meaning of that dreadful news would remember what he had been doing when the radio announcement shattered the Sunday peace. "Remember Pearl Harbor!" would become the rallying cry of a nation shocked and united in anger. As Franklin Roosevelt mapped war strategy with military chiefs and government officials, the attack reminded him of a comparable peril to the American republic. For a single sad moment he looked across the White House lawn. "From this same window," he said, "Lincoln watched the Confederate campfires twinkling across the Potomac."

At 12:30 P.M. on December 8, Roosevelt addressed an emergency session of Congress. In the House of Representatives that day there were no Democrats, no Republicans—only Americans angered to their souls by the Japanese attack, looking to their President for leadership. F.D.R. voiced the outrage and determination of a united America when he said:

Yesterday, December 7, 1941—a date that will live in infamy—the United States

Its signal flags still set, the U.S.S. California *slowly sinks at Pearl Harbor.*

127

of America was attacked by naval and air forces of the Empire of Japan. The United States was at peace with that nation. . . . Always will we remember the character of the attack against us. . . .

No matter how long it took America to revenge this "premeditated invasion," he said, the United States would win "absolute victory" and "make very certain that this form of treachery shall never endanger us again. . . . With confidence in our armed forces—with the unbounded determination of our people—we will gain the inevitable triumph—so help us God."

Then the President uttered the awesome, inevitable words: "I ask that the Congress declare that since the unprovoked and dastardly attack on Sunday, December Seventh, a state of war has existed between the United States and the Japanese Empire." After tumultuous cheers, Congress declared war on Japan with only one dissenting vote. Three days later, Germany and Italy declared war on the United States, fulfilling their pledge to Tokyo.

As the President set the American war machine in motion, the disaster deepened. With lightning speed, the Japanese attacked Hong Kong, Wake Island, Midway, Thailand. Tojo's vision of a Pacific empire was becoming a reality. Even the Philippines fell victim to wave after wave of amphibious assaults. Before Christmas MacArthur was forced to evacuate Manila and retreat to Bataan Penin-

sula and finally to Corregidor. His troops were surrounded and near starvation when, on March 11, MacArthur was ordered by the President to leave the Philippines. Pledging that he would return, he set up headquarters in Australia.

On April 9 Bataan fell to the Japanese and more than 12,000 Americans and 60,000 Filipinos surrendered. On May 6 Corregidor fell. Malaya fell, and Singapore, the Dutch East Indies, and after a three-day naval battle disastrous to the Allies, the island of Java. Australia and even the Aleutian Islands were threatened.

In the Atlantic the situation was no better. Between January and April, 1942, alone, nearly 200 ships were sunk by Nazi U-boats. In May and June 182 more were sunk in the straits of Florida, the Gulf of Mexico, and the Caribbean. U.S. vessels were torpedoed thirty miles off New York City, off Virginia Beach, and at the entrance to the Panama Canal. From Maine to Florida lights in coastal cities were blacked out for fear of submarine bombardment.

The war ultimately would leave more than 300,000 Americans dead and over 800,000 wounded. More than fifteen million would serve in the armed forces, including all eligible men between the ages of eighteen and forty-five, and more than 200,000 women in the Woman's Army Corps, the Waves, Spars, and Woman's Marine Corps. Six million unemployed Americans would finally find jobs when the government signed massive defense supply contracts with big business.

Much has been written, often accurately, about Roosevelt's divisive tactics as an administrator, his excessive reliance on his personal charm in getting things done, his delight in bypassing traditional government channels and overruling even his highest officials. But no one has justifiably questioned his astonishing courage and executive skill in facing what has been called "the greatest emergency in the history of mankind." Republicans and Democrats alike joined in praising his competence as a war leader, his capacity to instill confidence, to marshal the military, industrial, and civilian resources of America.

Undersecretary of State Sumner Welles recalled that even on Pearl Harbor day Roosevelt "demonstrated that ultimate capacity to dominate and to control a supreme emergency, which is perhaps the rarest and most valuable characteristic of any statesman. With complete grasp of every development, . . . the President never for one split second ceased to be master of the fate of his country," personally handling "every detail of the situation which his military and naval advisors laid before him." Despite his ingrained eagerness to be on top of things, F.D.R. completely trusted and delegated ultimate authority to the United States military command. Even during the D-Day landing at Normandy, wrote Army Chief of Staff George C. Marshall, Roosevelt "made

no request at any time for information other than that furnished him as a matter of routine. . . . The confidence he gave to the management of the Army was a tremendous source of assurance."

More than that, F.D.R. demonstrated a certain grasp of the revolutionary realities of modern warfare, especially in air power. As early as September, 1938, wrote Air Force General H. H. Arnold, Roosevelt saw the need for a massive strategic air command, "the first time in history we had ever had a program." Roosevelt's Republican Secretary of War, Henry L. Stimson, concluded that F.D.R. was "without exception the best war President the United States has ever had." Roosevelt refused to use his influence as Commander in Chief even to protect his sons from combat; all four of them fought in the war with valor and distinction. When a Republican Congressman rose in the House to charge the President with coddling his boys, Elliott wrote his father: "Pops, sometimes I really hope that one of us gets killed so that maybe they'll stop picking on the rest of the family."

Mobilizing American industry and labor for war, Roosevelt demonstrated the flair for experiment that had marked the early New Deal. He established the War Production Board, and in the words of its director, Donald Nelson, he gave it "complete responsibility for providing weapons with which to beat the Axis to its

TEXT CONTINUED ON PAGE 132

THE WASHINGTON HIGH COMMAND

President Roosevelt was more than anything else an inspiration to America during the second world war. He personified the nation's resolve to win. But it was the extraordinarily able team of civilians and military men that he gathered in Washington that guided the United States through the mobilization and oversaw the massive military effort. Indeed, so effectively did that team work together that it remained essentially unchanged throughout the war.

Henry Stimson was Secretary of War. He held Cabinet posts under four presidents.

Cordell Hull, a former Tennessee Senator, was Secretary of State for over a decade.

Edward R. Stettinius, Jr., ran Lend-Lease before being made Secretary of State.

Frank Knox, a Republican newspaper publisher, was made Secretary of the Navy.

James V. Forrestal was Undersecretary of the Navy before succeeding Knox in 1944.

A brilliant strategist, General George C. Marshall, above, was Army Chief of Staff.

Admiral William D. Leahy, right, became military chief of staff to the President.

Careful and experienced, Admiral Ernest J. King became Chief of Naval Operations.

General H. H. ("Hap") Arnold headed the Air Corps, then part of the U.S. Army.

TEXT CONTINUED FROM PAGE 129

knees." The WPB was perhaps the most powerful agency of the Roosevelt "alphabetocracy." It co-ordinated arms production nationwide; it mediated the often conflicting claims of the armed services; it helped greatly in stabilizing the civilian economy by the defense jobs it created. The Office of Civilian Defense co-ordinated efforts to meet an invasion of the United States by supervising blackouts and air raid drills.

The Office of Price Administration and later the Office of Economic Stabilization made valiant, if frequently unsuccessful attempts to hold down prices, fighting the inflationary pressures that invariably accompany a war. Rationing—something new to Americans on so vast a scale—discouraged hoarding and assured an adequate flow of scarce meat and butter, tires and gasoline to the armed forces. The Board of Economic Warfare regulated the stockpile of supplies essential to the war effort. The War Manpower Commission supervised the employment of Americans in positions of greatest value to the nation's strategic interests.

A vigorous program of American and Allied propaganda and psychological warfare was conducted by the Office of War Information. The CIA had its origin in the Office of Strategic Services, which trained secret agents and saboteurs, directly assisting the French Resistance movement, for example, in its underground battle against Hitler's puppet government in Paris. Greatly aided by the voluntary self-censorship of the American press, the Office of Censorship controlled the publication of war news and with extraordinary success saw to it that the movements of the President and the armed services remained completely secret.

Finally, material aid to nations fighting the Axis was increased greatly. Through "UNRRA"—the United Nations Relief and Rehabilitation Administration—four billion dollars worth of food, medicine, machinery, and other supplies, more than two thirds of them paid for by America, were dispatched to forty-eight nations between 1944 and 1947.

Not all of Roosevelt's wartime agencies were uniformly successful. Interservice or interdepartmental rivalry hampered some of them, and Harold Smith, the Director of the Budget from 1939 to 1946, estimated that perhaps five to seven per cent of the agencies foundered through inefficiency or misdirection. But he recalled in later years, "I can see in perspective the ninety-three or -four or -five per cent that went right—including the winning of the biggest war in history—because of unbelievably skillful organization and direction." Roo-

During the second world war American factories worked around the clock to produce some 300,000 military planes at a cost of $45 billion. Right, a seemingly endless row of SBD Dauntless dive bombers are assembled at a Douglas Aircraft Company plant.

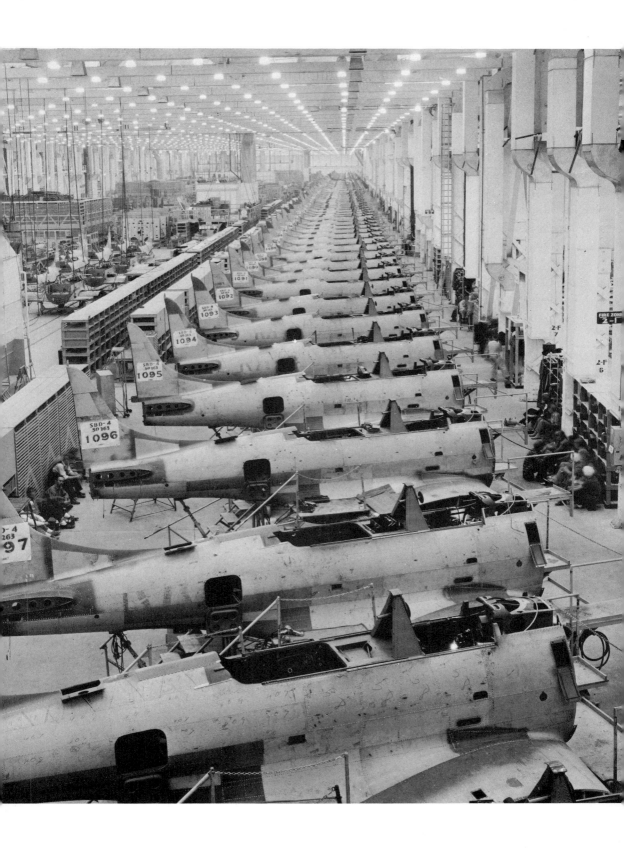

sevelt, he added appreciatively, "was a real *artist* in government."

The year 1943 marked the turning of the tide for the Allies. On January 5, after a tremendous struggle, the Nazis surrendered in the battle of Stalingrad, after the Russians had surrounded and destroyed almost their entire Sixth Army. On February 9, eight months after the decisive naval victory at Midway, the United States forced the Japanese to abandon Guadalcanal and pressed the attack against New Guinea, the Solomons, and Tarawa. It was the beginning of a systematic, island by island recovery of the Pacific to the very home waters of Japan. In mid-May, Nazi General Erwin Rommel's crack Afrika Korps was routed. Sicily was invaded in July, Italy in September. Hitler's "invincible" *Festung Europa* (European Fortress) had been breached. Allied victory seemed only a matter of time.

Roosevelt, meanwhile, waged a vigorous personal diplomatic war in

At the conclusion of their meeting in Casablanca, Morocco, in 1943 Roosevelt and Churchill announced that the Allies would accept only "unconditional surrender" from the Axis powers.

co-operation with his friend and ally Winston Churchill. On January 9, 1943, F.D.R. flew in secret to Casablanca, Morocco—his first plane trip since his dramatic flight to the Chicago convention in 1932. There he, Churchill, and Allied military chiefs planned the invasion of Sicily and Italy, and Allied aid to China was assured through the reopening of the famed "Burma Road." But the Casablanca conference is remembered chiefly for the dramatic announcement that the Allies would accept nothing less than "unconditional surrender" by the Axis powers. Rexford Tugwell, a key Roosevelt brain-truster, conceded years later that this decision "has been increasingly regarded since as the most serious political error of the war." It has been argued that by leaving no door open to moderates in Germany and Japan who might have sued for an early peace, the Allied policy of "unconditional surrender" only strengthened the enemy's resolve to fight to the bitter end.

Hitler's insane refusal to admit defeat from his bombarded bunker in Berlin and Japan's suicide "kamikaze" air assaults on U.S. vessels support this view. Moreover, the Casablanca announcement's tone of "revenge and punishment," as Rexford Tugwell observes, struck many as "poor beginnings of work for peace." On the other hand, it can be argued that the memory of Pearl Harbor was still fresh and that the Allied desire for revenge against the Nazis increased irreversi-

bly as word of Hitler's incredible, systematic annihilation of millions of Jews, Poles, and others leaked out.

Roosevelt met Churchill again in Cairo on November 23, 1943, joined this time by Chiang Kai-shek. The principal object was to map strategy in the war against Japan. A few days later, at Teheran, Roosevelt, Churchill, and Marshal Stalin made further plans in the war against Germany. (Italy had surrendered two months earlier.) Roosevelt had never met the Soviet dictator, and from all accounts, the two leaders hit it off very well—so very well that by the end of the conference, F.D.R. was calling the Marshal Uncle Joe.

Momentous decisions were made at Teheran. "Operation Overlord," the long-awaited Allied invasion of Europe on the French coast, would take place in June, 1944, and would be led by General Dwight D. Eisenhower. Stalin agreed to press the Nazis more vigorously on the Eastern Front, engaging then, as before, the overwhelming strength of Hitler's armies. He also agreed to declare war on Japan six months after Germany surrendered—enough time for Russia to redeploy its armies. Plans also were made for the partition of Germany into zones occupied by the various Allies.

Roosevelt, however, was preoccupied with more than military issues. As Eisenhower said later, "while [F.D.R.] recognized the seriousness of the war problems still facing the Allies,

Japan's downfall was planned in July, 1944, at Honolulu by F.D.R. and his commanders: Admiral Chester Nimitz (at map), General Douglas MacArthur (left), and Admiral Leahy.

much of his comment dealt with the distant future, the post-hostilities tasks, . . ." in short, with the kind of peace and world order that alone could justify the Allies' huge expenditures in human life and resources. At Teheran, Roosevelt discussed the critical need for a working union of independent nations with the power to police the peace—a union especially of the U.S., the United Kingdom, the U.S.S.R., and China. This "committee of the whole," the President argued, would renounce the use of force among them, share resources, and in

Tugwell's words, "provide the common means for stifling conflict before it became dangerous."

It is clear that neither Stalin nor Churchill shared the idealistic vision of the President, who had learned the lessons of his old patron Woodrow Wilson, after all. It is also clear that neither Stalin nor Churchill knew the secret that had convinced Roosevelt that in the postwar world the "Big Four" could choose only between coexistence or coextermination. In December, 1942, the United States had set off the world's first self-sustaining nuclear reaction; the fateful advent of the atom bomb was not far off.

The Teheran conferees settled for a lofty statement. They said that they recognized fully "the supreme responsibility resting upon us and all the nations to make a peace which will . . . banish the scourge and terror of war for many generations. . . . We shall seek the cooperation and active participation of all nations, large and small . . . whose peoples are dedicated to the elimination of tyranny. . . ." If America and the Soviet Union remained allies in peace as they had in war, Roosevelt thought, what nation would possess the strength to begin another world war? On Christmas Eve, 1943, Roosevelt announced optimistically in a fireside chat to the nation: "I may say that I 'got along fine' with Marshal Stalin, . . . and I believe that we are going to get along very well with him and the Russian people —very well indeed."

On June 6, 1944, as American forces closed in on Japan and the Russian army smashed toward Germany, the largest amphibious force ever assembled invaded the French coast at

After the Cairo and Teheran conferences, Roosevelt named Eisenhower Commander in Chief of Allied Forces in Western Europe. Below, they confer during a stopover in Sicily.

Normandy. The long awaited D-Day began at 6:30 A.M. Under cover of eleven thousand planes, six hundred warships and four thousand other vessels landed wave after wave of Allied troops—155,000 men in all. "The tide has turned," General Eisenhower proclaimed. "The free men of the world are marching together to victory." At

home, President Roosevelt went on the radio and led all Americans in the deeply moving "D-Day Prayer" that he had written:

Almighty God: Our sons . . . this day have set upon a mighty endeavor, a struggle to preserve our Republic, our religion, and our civilization, and to set free a suffering

On D-Day the Allies assaulted the heavily fortified coast of Normandy at five points code-named Utah, Omaha, Gold, Juno, and Sword. By nightfall, they held a beachhead sixty miles long and ten miles deep.

humanity. . . . They fight not for the lust of conquest. . . . They fight to liberate. . . . They yearn but for the end of battle, for their return to the haven of home. Some will never return. Embrace these, Father, and receive them, Thy heroic servants, into Thy Kingdom. . . .

By June 12, the Allies had disembarked over 300,000 men and 50,000 vehicles, breaching the "Atlantic Wall" that Hitler had declared impenetrable. On other fronts, too, the Axis powers suffered major setbacks. On June 15, American superfortresses began massive air attacks against the Japanese home islands. By mid-July, the Nazis conceded that Russian forces had advanced to the very "gates of the Reich!" in East Prussia. On July 18, after American troops had taken the strategic island of Saipan, Japan's Premier Hideki Tojo resigned in disgrace.

The news from all war fronts was good, but at home, F.D.R. faced another challenge: the Presidential election of 1944. In late June the Republicans had nominated New York's urbane, politically astute Governor, Thomas E. Dewey, as their candidate. He was a proven vote-getter, still riding on his reputation as a racket-busting district attorney. The Democrats nominated Roosevelt, by acclamation, for a fourth term. Bowing to conservative pressure, they dropped the increasingly left-of-center Henry Wallace and named the more moderate Senator Harry S. Truman of Missouri as F.D.R.'s running mate.

The Republicans, with Dewey's tacit approval, waged a scurrilous, personal campaign against the President. Despite Pearl Harbor and *Mein Kampf,* they said the war was "Roosevelt's war"; he had provoked the Axis. As they had done in 1940, they attacked the President as a warmonger, on the one hand, and as guilty of inadequate American military preparedness, on the other. Dewey himself repeatedly assailed the "tired old men" of the Roosevelt Administration, declaring that it was "time for a change." The Republicans questioned the President's patriotism by suggesting that he was being ruled by such "foreign-born" radicals as union chief Sidney Hillman, who, they charged, was a close ally of Earl Browder, chief of the U.S. Communist Party. Again the whispering campaign was launched: Roosevelt was sick, the rumors went, he no longer was able to function effectively.

Preoccupied with the war effort and no doubt confident that he would be re-elected, Roosevelt decided early in the campaign to make few speeches. He clearly feared the effects on American wartime unity of a bitter, narrowly partisan fight. When the polls showed Dewey gaining, however, Roosevelt entered the ring. In a September address to the Teamsters'

In 1944 Roosevelt's Republican opponent was Thomas E. Dewey, Governor of New York—simply "that little man" to F.D.R.

Roosevelt, Vice-President-elect Harry S. Truman(center), and outgoing Vice-President Henry A. Wallace returned to Washington damp but jubilant after the 1944 election returns were in.

Union, he seized upon an absurd charge made against him by a Republican Congressman to reduce Dewey to a ridicule from which he never wholly escaped.

These Republican leaders [Roosevelt declared with solemn glee] have not been content with attacks on me, or my wife, or on my sons. . . . they now include my little dog, Fala. Well, of course, I don't resent attacks, and my family doesn't resent attacks, but Fala *does* resent them. You know, Fala is Scotch, and being a Scottie, as soon as he learned that the Republican fiction writers . . . had concocted a story that I had left him behind on the Aleutian Islands and had sent a destroyer back to find him—at a cost to the taxpayers of two or three, or eight or twenty million dollars—his Scotch soul was furious. He has not been the same dog since.

To counter attacks on his health, F.D.R. toured four boroughs of New York City just before the election. An estimated three million people turned out to greet him as he rode in an open car through a wind-swept rain, waving and grinning, chilled to the bone.

Dewey was an internationalist like Willkie, and he, too, was hurt by the isolationists and right-wing extremists in his party. Roosevelt was quick to seize on the split. Claiming the support of millions of Republicans, Roosevelt declared that the issues of war and peace were above partisan politics and he asked the nation to vote accordingly. As the campaign drew to a close, he had made the coming world order under the United Nations the central issue of the campaign, warning, however, that peace could not be maintained unless the U.N. was empowered to keep it by force if necessary. In a radio talk from Hyde Park on the eve of the election, the President warned that another war "would be bound to bring even more devilish and powerful instruments of destruction to wipe out civilian populations" than Hitler's new long-range rocket bombs, which had gutted London. "No coastal defenses," he warned, "however strong, could prevent these silent missiles of death, fired perhaps from planes or ships at sea, from crashing deep within the United States itself."

"This time, this time," the President declared, "we must be certain that the peace-loving nations of the world band together in determination to outlaw and to prevent war." In the age of the H-bomb and the intercontinental missile, Roosevelt's warning assumes a new poignancy.

Roosevelt defeated Dewey by a margin of over three and a half million popular votes—25,606,585 to 22,014,745—and an Electoral College landslide of 432 to 99. When Dewey refused to offer the President the traditional congratulations, Roosevelt's temper flared. He always had dismissed Dewey contemptuously as "that little man." Now he fired off a parting shot: "I still think he's a son of a bitch."

The fourth term race in 1944 [Jimmy Roosevelt recalled] was Father's death warrant. I saw him only twice during that period. . . . Each time I realized with awful, irrevocable certainty that we were going to lose him. I think Father himself both knew it, and with that indomitable buoyancy—and stubbornness—of his, refused to know it.

It was, indeed, a changed Franklin Roosevelt who stood on the south portico of the White House on January 20, 1945, to take the Presidential oath for the fourth time. Hatless and coatless in the bitter cold, he looked suddenly old and fearfully tired. The Allies had broken the back of Nazi resistance at the Battle of the Bulge, but only after 100,000 Allies and Germans had been killed. MacArthur had returned in triumph to the Philippines. But the war was far from over, and in keeping with the nation's somber wartime mood, the President had asked that the inauguration ceremonies be simple and brief.

In his final inaugural address, the President recited again the lesson of

Pearl Harbor and Normandy Beach. "We have learned," he said, "that we cannot live alone, at peace; that our own well-being is dependent on the well-being of other nations far away. We have learned that we must live as men, not as ostriches. . . ."

In this spirit, Roosevelt journeyed to his fateful conference with Stalin and Churchill at Yalta, in the Crimea, on February 5, 1945. His primary military objective was to secure Russia's entry into the war against Japan, for he and his advisors, including General Douglas MacArthur, were convinced that a bloody invasion of the Japanese home islands was inevitable. Japan's fanatical military tactics—notably its "kamikaze" suicide air raids and its orders to its troops to fight to the death—made it clear that American losses would be painfully high. Russian assistance appeared essential, particularly since the atomic bomb had not yet come to the testing stage.

Accordingly, in exchange for Stalin's agreement to enter the war against Japan, broad territorial and political concessions were made to the Soviet dictator, concessions that plunged America into political controversy from which it has not recovered yet. The Soviets were given southern Sakhalin Island and the Kuriles. Russia's "pre-eminent interests" in Manchuria were recognized. Eastern Poland was given to Stalin when the dictator promised to hold free elections. Roosevelt and Churchill acceded still further to Stalin's wishes by agreeing that "coalition" governments of Communists and non-Communists might be set up in several Eastern European nations, also pending free elections.

Roosevelt acted less in ignorance of emerging Soviet designs on Eastern Europe—as his subsequent angry correspondence with Stalin shows—than on the basis of several tragically mistaken predictions. Military intelligence overestimated the strength on the home islands of the Japanese army, which by then had been reduced to a token force. The atom bomb would be ready much sooner than expected, eliminating the need for Soviet help. But even Roosevelt's most ardent admirers have to admit that the President acted partly out of titanic conceit. He believed he could handle "Uncle Joe" through sheer personal charm, as he had handled Democratic precinct chieftains and political favor-seekers during more than two decades of political life. His approach to the Soviet Union as a reliable ally, despite the Communist blueprint for international revolution and world empire, at least as old as Lenin, bordered on innocence.

The ailing President could take some consolation from Stalin's agreement to enter the United Nations, the organization that Roosevelt believed would be the supreme achievement of his life. It was agreed at Yalta that the U.N. would meet at San Francisco on April 25, 1945, taking its first steps

Roosevelt last met Churchill and Stalin in February, 1945, at a week-long conference in Yalta. Before the Allied leaders posed for a formal portrait, a photographer snapped this picture.

144

"to prevent aggression and to remove the political, economic and social causes of war through the close and continuing collaboration of all peace-loving peoples."

Franklin Roosevelt would not live to see the United Nations founded. He had lost a great deal of weight; his eyes were ringed and puffed with age; he was, in fact, very ill. Churchill recalled that at Yalta F.D.R. had "seemed placid and frail. I felt that he had a slender contact with life." Addressing a special session of Congress on March 1, 1945, to ask its support for the United Nations, Roosevelt broke his long silence about the polio that had crippled him twenty-four years before. He spoke sitting down and asked Congress' pardon for his "unusual posture." His braces were heavy, he said. He was exhausted after his 14,000-mile journey to Yalta and the Middle East. But he had come with an urgent, an imperative message. After World War I, the President said, "American fighting men looked to the statesmen of the world to finish the work of peace for which they fought and suffered. We failed them. We failed them then. We cannot fail them again, and expect the world to survive."

On April 12, 1945, Franklin Roosevelt's four sons, away at war, received a message from their mother. Elliott was at an air base in England; John and Franklin, Jr., "somewhere in the Pacific"; and Jimmy in the Philippines. The message was brief:

145

On his doctors' orders, the President had gone to his beloved Warm Springs for a much-needed rest. Important, even historic events lay ahead: Roosevelt planned to appear at the opening session of the United Nations; he had mail to answer, a special U.N. stamp to approve, a Jefferson Day speech to hone to a fine edge. At 1:15 P.M. on April 12, while sitting for a portrait and dictating correspondence, Franklin Roosevelt collapsed. "I have a terrific headache," he whispered before falling into a coma. He died at 3:35 P.M. from a cerebral hemorrhage. The official bulletin announced, with moving simplicity: "ARMY-NAVY DEAD: Roosevelt, Franklin D., Commander in Chief."

With military victory in sight and a new world organization about to be born, F.D.R. had died, as the distinguished American poet Archibald MacLeish wrote:

> Fagged out, worn down, sick
> With the weight of his own bones, the
>   task finished,
> The war won, the victory assured,
> The glory left behind him for the
>   others. . . .

When the President's cortege left Warm Springs, his fellow patients, lined up in their wheelchairs, waved a last silent good-by. In tears, Graham Jackson, a favorite accordionist, played "Going Home." The Presidential train, bearing the Commander in Chief's body, moved slowly past sorrowful crowds in Georgia, the Carolinas, and Virginia to Washington. In American cities and towns millions wept openly in the streets. Asked if she had heard the news by radio, a housewife replied: "For what do I need a radio? It's on everybody's face." A Harlem resident calmed his grieving neighbors: "Don't worry. He was a great man with great ideas. . . . His plans are made and somebody's gonna carry them out."

After a state funeral service in the White House, F.D.R. made his final journey up the Hudson. To the roll of muffled drums his flag-draped coffin was carried on an Army caisson up the hill to his home at Hyde Park. Guns roared the nation's final tribute as Franklin Delano Roosevelt was buried in the Rose Garden on Sunday, April 15.

"The spring was just showing as the year turned toward life from the death of winter," wrote F.D.R.'s old New Deal friend, Rexford Tugwell. "The aged trees Franklin had climbed as a boy were just in bud and the roses had not yet bloomed, but the grass of the lawns was green in the chilly air. The place was sweet and close as it would always be."

As the train bearing the body of F.D.R. left Warm Springs, Chief Petty Officer Graham Jackson played "Going Home."

146

Half a year before he died, F. D. R. took his famous friend Fala for a spin in the autumn sunshine at the family's Hyde Park estate.

ACKNOWLEDGMENTS

The Editors would like to thank the following individuals and organizations for their valuable assistance:

Franklin Delano Roosevelt Library, Hyde Park—Paul McLaughlin
Audre Proctor

AMERICAN HERITAGE
JUNIOR LIBRARY

Kenneth W. Leish, *Editor*

Alfred Mayor, *Managing Editor*

Harriet S. Cole, *Art Director*

Sandra L. Russell, *Copy Editor*

Jessica Bourgeois, *Picture Editor*

Susan Eikov, *Text Researcher*

Annette Jarman, *Editorial Assistant*

The Editors would also like to acknowledge the following sources: The quotations on pages 29, 34, 39, 65, 79, and 142 are from *Affectionately, F.D.R.*, by James Roosevelt and Sidney Shalett, published by Harcourt, Brace & World, Inc., 1959. The quotation on pages 36–37 is from *Reilly of the White House,* © 1947 by Michael F. Reilly and William J. Slocum, and is reprinted by permission of Simon & Schuster, Inc. The quotations on pages 83 and 89–90 are from Volumes II and III of *The Age of Roosevelt,* by Arthur M. Schlesinger, Jr., published by Houghton Mifflin Company, 1958, 1960. The quotation on page 146 is from *Actfive and Other Poems,* by Archibald Macleish, published by Random House, Inc., 1948.

FURTHER REFERENCE

The Home of Franklin D. Roosevelt at Hyde Park, New York, is now a National Historic Site open to the public daily except Christmas from 9 A.M. to 5 P.M. Among the rooms on view are F.D.R.'s bedroom and the office and bedroom he used while he was President; the living room, dining room, and main hall, all of them furnished as they were when the Roosevelts lived there. Not far from the house is the Franklin D. Roosevelt Library, containing the millions of papers of President and Mrs. Roosevelt and materials relating to their private lives and special interests. The research room is open Monday through Friday excluding holidays from 9 A.M. to 5 P.M. to those who have made written application and been granted permission by the Director to use the collections. Also in the Library is a Museum, open to all from 9 A.M. to 5 P.M. daily except Christmas. It contains personal belongings of President Roosevelt's, gifts he received, and objects he collected, as well as the study from which he delivered several of his radio speeches. The exhibitions are changed from time to time. The Site's 187 acres of grounds are open every day until sundown, admission free. An admission fee of 50 cents is charged by the Museum of the Library, admission to the research room is free, and admission to the Home is 50 cents. Persons under 16 are admitted free to both the Library Museum and the Home.

The following books are recommended for further reading:

Churchill, Allen, *The Roosevelts, American Aristocrats.* Harper & Row, 1965.

Freidel, Frank, *Franklin D. Roosevelt*, five vols. Little, Brown, 1952, 1954, 1956, 1958, 1964.

Leuchtenburg, William E., *Franklin D. Roosevelt and the New Deal.* Harper & Row, 1963.

Moley, Raymond, *The First New Deal.* Harcourt, Brace, 1966.

Rollins, Alfred B., Jr., *Roosevelt and Howe.* Knopf, 1962.

Roosevelt, Eleanor, *The Autobiography of Eleanor Roosevelt.* Harper, 1961.

Roosevelt, James, and Shalett, Sidney. *Affectionately, F.D.R.* Harcourt, Brace, 1959.

Schlesinger, Arthur M., Jr., *The Age of Roosevelt*, three vols. Houghton Mifflin, 1957, 1958, 1960.

Sherwood, Robert E., *Roosevelt and Hopkins: An Intimate History*, revised ed., Harper, 1950.

Tugwell, Rexford G., *The Democratic Roosevelt.* Penguin, 1969 (paperback).

Roosevelt campaigning for a second term in Jamestown, North Dakota

INDEX

Boldface indicates pages on which illustrations appear.

153